1

KILIMANJARO – TALES FROM THE HIGH LIFE
'Mr Mountain Man'

© R Binout

To: travel companions past, present and future.

Dedicated to: Uncle Colin, father-in-law Joe, Auntie June, Uncle Peter, Uncle Ralph and cousin Sally.

Special thanks to: Mum & Dad for a lifetime of unconditional support, to Kate for invaluable advice and unorthodox editing techniques, and to the long-suffering but always supportive Mrs Binout and our two most precious offspring who have to endure my excessive desire to get out and explore. And, of course, thanks Matt, I couldn't have done it without you.

Author: R Binout

Editor: Kate Warsop

CONTENTS

KILIMANJARO – TALES FROM THE HIGH LIFE
'Mr Mountain Man'

Prologue

When I returned home from my trip to Tanzania, I quickly referred to my travel diary notes in order to write a fuller account of my experiences before the vivid memories faded. Out of those friends and family members who could be bothered (or felt obliged) to read my personal journal, I received many unprompted and unincentivised complimentary comments and some even suggested that I should publish my story. Naturally, I was extremely flattered but, at that time, I had no idea how to bring such an undertaking to the publication stage.

However, over the past few years I have become involved in editorial work as well as learning all about the necessary procedures required to self-publish. And, always at the back of my mind has been my Kilimanjaro story. So, armed with relevant experience and recently acquired confidence, and no small amount of encouragement, I've finally written and published this *ripping yarn*.

It's only fair to state that the bare branches of this tale have been foliated to varying degrees. I make no excuse for extrapolation, exaggeration or tangential meanderings because I want this story to entertain and inspire. Names, characters, and some details (for personal and privacy reasons) have been changed but rest assured, everything you read is based upon truth, fact and real circumstances.

Chapter 1 – Day 2. (Plenty of) Time for reflection...

If you've ever endured the night in a tent in a bucolic location then you might appreciate that one of life's simpler luxuries is blissfully sleeping in your cosily accommodating bed, in a warm room, with the bathroom nearby. In fact, it's not only, oh so comforting to be able to casually throw back the duvet and shuffle instinctively into the bathroom in the dark but then you might also discover that you have the added bonus of it being the early hours of the morning in which case you still have the luxury of several more hours of dreamy, oblivious sleep ahead before it's time to embark upon the new day.

Today? No such bloody luck!

Following the earlier disturbances, sinister noises, snoring from 'The Beast', highly frustrating attempts to sleep and a visit to the team toilet, my bladder, once again, announced its capacity had, annoyingly, very nearly reached overflowing, dripping-in-the-pants, point. It would have been so convenient, pleasing in fact, to have found my headtorch lying down next to my side but of course, it wasn't. I considered remaining in my snuggled state for just a tiny weeny little bit longer. It was probably only shortly before we needed to get up anyway.

However, fit to burst bladders tend to trump everything and this occasion was no exception. I apologised to Matt, my brother-in-law, whom I knew was only dozing, sat upright and continued my fumbling quest for the illuminating grail.

I fondled a fleece which I thought I might as well put on, a water bottle, three 'stuff sacks', and my toiletries bag. Finally, I located the torch and strapped it onto my head. Enlightened, I couldn't wait to show Matt.

Bugger! My watch brought the disheartening news that it was only a quarter past three. I'd convinced myself it was surely approaching breakfast time.

I then committed the night time cardinal sin of shining my dazzlingly bright headlight directly into Matt's eyes as I turned to talk to him. Come on, we've all done it, haven't we? Anyway, in response to the fully warranted and, I must say, rather impressive range of expletives - Matt has a unique way with words, especially at jolly early o'clock - I adjusted the white-light beam to shine upwards. My tent-mate's swearing soon morphed into forthright 'advice': it has to be said, still including a palette of colourful expletives, some of which, may even have been in Swahili. Honestly, some people are so touchy.

"We all need people who will give us feedback. That's how we improve." – Bill Gates. Hmm Bill? In a dignified, air-conditioned office environment, within a company making obscene profits and with perfectly understandable English being spoken, I'm with you all the way, mate. But, in a tent, granted a cosy one, with Matt as company, heaving with obscene language and a looming emergency bladder situation, I'm not so sure that 'feedback' was what I really needed at that exact moment.

However, to be fair, this led to me fiddling about with a dial and discovering a rather gentle blue-light setting. Far less obtrusive. Matt's extremely blunt but nevertheless very useful 'feedback' had helped restore the calmness within our cosy tent. An early-trip 'domestic' had been neatly dodged, we'd come through it together and it had possibly bonded us just a little closer. Well, that's how I viewed it, literally, in this new light. I'm not sure about Matt. I'd like to think he was only half-pretending to be grumpy. However, this wasn't the time to dwell on our 'relationship'. My attention quickly refocused.

With my bladder bulging like a sun-ripened water melon on a tropical island market stall but without the succulent appeal, I quickly unzipped the sleeping bag, pulled on my trousers, struggled into my soft daps - a pair of rubber-soled, canvas shoes I'd bought for less than a tenner, purely for this trip to wear whenever I was in camp in order to give my feet a break from my hiking boots - and, after catching my breath, unzipped the tent flaps.

My determination was immediately deflated, unlike my sloshing bladder, as a glowing light shone through the blue canvas of our team toilet tent. No 'engaged' sign was required. So, I could either have waited for it to become vacant, go behind a tree or try the nearby Big Tree Camp's 'long-drop' toilet.

The first option would have involved pacing around the immediate vicinity coughing and breathing heavily in a way to announce my presence whilst, at the same time, surely becoming an irresistible beacon and landing platform for ungainly flapping monstrous moths drawn to the radiance of my bulbous head light.

The second one: going behind a tree? Because I was in a creepy crawly-infested jungle environment in the dark *all by myself*, was obviously not an option worthy of a moment's consideration, full stop! *Seeing* these unfamiliar potential foes in daylight is scary enough in itself. But, only being able to *hear* 'them' at night time, waiting for an inevitable sting, bite or a wrapping around my torso with crushing might, was too horrendous to contemplate.

There was, of course, no real choice. It was going to have to be the 'long-drop'. Should all be fairly straightforward though?

My anxious bladder entered first with me very close behind shuffling cautiously across the wooden floor. I didn't really know what to fully expect. I'd not seen a single manual on 'long-drop' toilets so felt surprised, after only a couple of tentative paces or so, to be confronted with a left turn and an almost immediate doubling back on myself.

My right foot then failed to land on anything solid as there seemed to be a hole in the floor. I inevitably fell crashing forward. My right hand instinctively reached out successfully grabbing at a cross timber which lessened the blow as my head hit the side of the toilet's structure sending my headtorch flying. Fortunately, it sounded as though it had landed softly.

In a strange crouched position, perhaps reminiscent of a tai chi routine and with my right foot dangling ominously like some form of live bait sensing imminent peril, I wriggled around in the gloom quickly regained my balance together with a semblance of dignity.

My pants, which I'd slightly wet in the mayhem, were the first obvious casualty. Being a man approaching 'a certain age', I accepted this dribbling seepage with mild resignation.

I recovered the headtorch but quickly discovered that it too, like my pants, was also a tad tarnished having landed in someone's misplaced excrement that lay silently in an expressionless heap on the floor. This 'heap' appeared to be goading me. That was definitely not acceptable!

Despite its decorative faecal embellishment, and controlling my gag reflex, I managed to switch the light back to its original bright setting.

Now surveying my surroundings, I could see that my lower leg had partly disappeared down the hole meant to be stood or squatted over. Aha, so that actually was the 'toilet'. Fortunately, my foot had not ended up in anything nasty as it really did appear to be a long drop, hence the name I presumed. I swiftly rescued my limb from its concerning dangle over the dark silent abyss.

The thought of the pit bottom's contents made my stomach churn. Now, perilously close to the murky muck, my heightened imagination ran amok. I half expected a hideous mutant jungle sewer creature to grab my leg and pull me in. If there was indeed one, it didn't. Perhaps it was still slowly digesting the previous clumsy visitor?

The 'hole in the floor' was oval-shaped and, as I'd proved, was big enough to swallow a size-9 hiking boot. Either side of the hole were two small pieces of wood which I guessed were 'guides' for placing one's feet alongside before establishing a squatting position. Three randomly placed human turds then completed the 'long-drop's' 'flooral' display.

I suppose in the UK we're largely protected from potentially dangerous holes in the ground by sundry barriers, warning signs, over-zealous

Health and Safety laws and endless Risk Assessments; not so in a 'long-drop' toilet in Tanzania. For once, and only very briefly, I appreciated my nanny state.

My visual senses had seen quite enough. It was time to fully appreciate the 'flooral' bouquet. The oval-shaped hole had a perfectly matching oval-shaped dark damp stain around it. Clearly, this wasn't *Ronseal's* indoor *Quick Dry Woodstain Satin - Dark Oak* finish. It was, judging by its appearance and aroma, a urine-based permanently damp wood stain, more matt than satin finish, certainly not something one would want to be sat in but let's gloss over that. On a positive note, its 'old ammonia' bouquet partially disguised the wafts of a more putrid, slowly-decaying 'finish' rising reekingly from the 'pit' depths below.

It wasn't too long before I became acutely aware of why I was standing in this awful place. So, once again a zip was unfastened and I finally emptied my thankful bladder, still half expecting a gruesome rotting hand to rise menacingly up through the hole and drag me down into the dark sticky bowels of its rotten lair. Again, it didn't.

With my imagination beginning to settle and shock subsiding, I gingerly made my way back to the tent only this time with the torch light shining on the ground immediately in front of me. I wanted to make absolutely sure I could see where my feet were treading.

My *inaugural encounter* with a 'long-drop' toilet was over. In all honesty, it probably could have gone better. But hey, I'd travelled to Africa expecting new experiences and, on that account, it hadn't disappointed in the slightest.

Matt, naturally, offered no sympathy whatsoever. In fact, he found the whole episode highly amusing which, to be fair, so did I once I was safely cocooned in my sleeping bag.

One thing was becoming quickly apparent and that was the effect altitude was having on making nearly every, even the dullest situation seem rather funny. It was a wonderfully bizarre and infectious state of mind to be able to laugh with true abandon.

Before endeavouring to sleep, I faffed around opening a procession of stuff sacks in an attempt to find my invaluable, absolutely essential on a mountain trip, biodegradable wet wipes. Despite presumably leaving a trail of excreta on most of my bags from what I'd 'picked up' during the shocking but thankfully brief 'long-drop encounter', I did eventually find them, was relieved to wipe everything and, hopefully, disinfected all that was contaminated to, approaching, medically approved standards.

Feeling comforted, chuffed and now 'toilet-trained' in the dark damp dingy underworld of the Dark Arts of the Long-Drop, I lay down to enjoy a thoroughly well-deserved sleep.

But...

...that's not how it works on the first night of an exciting expedition for someone so ridiculously out of his comfort zone.

I lay there thinking that, *surely*, the next time I rolled over it would lead to sleep.

It didn't.

Consequently, it became an opportunity for frustration and reflection...

Only six months previously, a friend had asked whether I was planning anything for my looming landmark birthday. I excitedly announced that I would be hosting a 1970s themed party and... well, that was about it.

That night I lay in bed and realised I was at risk of becoming a boring old fart – I was effectively turning into my father; only kidding Dad. Admittedly friends and 'well-wishers' had been alluding to it for some time but now even I'd reached the same conclusion. Perhaps I really was drifting towards Old Fartdom. I could surely do better than just a big fancy dress party. Couldn't I? Could I?

After giving myself a thoroughly good talking to, and with 'YOLO' (something my kids often said and, I confess, I eventually asked them, with slight embarrassment, what they were on about) echoing around my mind, I recalled a long-ago Christmas present: the *1970 Guinness Book of Records*.

As a child, I remember being completely captivated by the contents of the book - the highest and lowest points on Earth, Robert Earl Hughes - the world's heaviest person and some bloke with impossibly long, curly finger nails. How could he possibly pick his nose or 'wipe' himself? I used to spend hours repeatedly poring over these incredible feats and freaks.

Whilst lay in bed excitedly pondering new possibilities, inspiration from the book flowed in a frenzy and the adrenalin surge was so ferocious that it brought on a rapid bowel movement. The very-much-taken-for-granted ensuite with a pristine clean floor was conveniently nearby. I adopted a very-much-taken-for-granted comfortable, relaxed, totally chilled sitting position *on a toilet seat* and enthusiastically contemplated my own Guinness-worthy adventure in my familiar brightly lit comfortable environment with soft velvety luxury toilet paper to hand. In fact, it was just the 'usual' toilet experience that I was completely accustomed to... all toilets are like that, aren't they?

Back in bed, I vowed that I too would attempt something extraordinary by my ordinary standards.

I immediately eliminated growing long finger nails as, for many reasons, it just seemed so impractical.

Next to be struck off was exploring the lower underwater regions of our planet. I'm not too keen on what lurks beneath the surface of the sea. I've seen far too many, admittedly fascinating, documentaries featuring the most fearfully ugly marine creatures aimlessly loitering with emotionless eyes and Botox faces just ready to pounce. (Rather like current day 'cougars.') In fact, when I was much younger, the seemingly innocuous underwater 'baddies' on *Stingray* used to keep me awake at night as did, much to my embarrassment today, Marina, who I rated as a bit of a babe despite the obvious shortcomings of her being a puppet; a relationship with her would surely have come with strings attached.

And finally, with ubiquitous sugary, fizzy drinks, and fast food chains on every high street, turning into a bed-ridden sizeable porker, like Robert Earl Hughes, appeared far too easy. The majority of people these days seemed to be participating in that particular feast of a feat.

So, Mount Everest it was then! That would undoubtedly put a sweaty hiking sock in the gaping mouths of my Doubting Thomas so-called friends. Yeah, I'll show 'em.

Dawn brought with it the sobering realisation that scrambling up to the highest point on Earth was totally unrealistic, that is, unless I had £30,000 sitting wantonly in my bank account, was extremely fit, had all the gear and didn't mind queuing up, for an hour or so in minus 50 degrees, behind 'mountain tourists' taking numerous selfies on that final stretch to the summit.

It was then I remembered a conversation in a pub many years before about Mount Kilimanjaro – the alluring highest point on the African continent in Tanzania - and how it was accessible to the average person but, nevertheless, posed a potentially gruelling and worthy challenge.

I'm sure I'd said on several occasions, after a few pints, that I'd tackle it one day; the usual beer talk. That was it though - Kilimanjaro! I felt really pleased that I'd finally reached a suitable conclusion with myself and was delighted that I'd agreed to it by way of a structured thought process and unanimous decision. Motion passed! I was going to climb Kilimanjaro... probably.

I announced my momentous decision to my incredulous family on Boxing Day. "Surely he's had too much bucks fizz?" I could read on their faces.

Everyone around the table had seen the 2009 *Red Nose Comic Relief* Celebrity Climb (The *Comic Relief* British charity commenced in 1985, with the idea to use comedy to raise money and change lives in Africa and the UK.) – it was the largest charity challenge event ever organised to conquer Kilimanjaro's summit. Prompted initially by an idea from singer, songwriter, musician Gary Barlow, a BT-sponsored team of eight celebrities, also including fellow music industry celebrities Ronan Keating and Cheryl Cole, embarked upon the challenge. The event eventually raised a whopping £3.5m, part of which went towards the goal of providing an anti-malaria net to every child under five in Tanzania.

The whole trip was broadcast by the BBC and watched by millions of viewers in the UK. The TV cameras had followed their every step and the resultant programme provided a very insightful and, at times, stark impression of what might be involved, including the fatigue, the puking, the dreaded altitude sickness and a hide-behind-the-sofa syringe moment.

Once the tumbleweed had cleared from the dining room and the shock subsided, the well-intentioned interrogation began. I have to admit that my plan (if I even had one) at that stage was very much in its infancy so I fielded the questions with very few precise details, much teenage-like shoulder shrugging and quite a few "dunnos".

With the wind rather taken out of my sails and the foundations of my expedition crumbling before ever having been launched, brother-in-law Matt quickly came to my rescue by announcing that he'd always wanted to climb Kilimanjaro and would be delighted to join me. What's more, as he'd not yet had a drink, it was obviously a statement of intent that hadn't been influenced by alcohol.

So that was that. No backing out now. The trip had been effectively witnessed and rubber-stamped. Matt and I *would* be climbing one of the highest most famous mountains in the world.

Whereas everything I knew about great outdoorsy activities could be written on the back of three first class stamps, that very same philatelic value would not have been anywhere near sufficient 'postage' to have delivered the comprehensive manuscript that Matt could have written on the subject. His renowned hiking and fieldcraft capabilities combined with his magnanimous declaration to join the trip had just guaranteed my success… hadn't it?

With summiting Kilimanjaro now assured, as well as it being the festive period, I had no desire to immediately begin the process of getting mountain fit. Instead, I enjoyed a trough of my Mum's legendary homemade mince pies, a lovely chilled bottle of Gavi, devoured the cheeseboard selection with some Taylor's vintage port and then decided it was time to commence the all-important, and thankfully not at all physically demanding, online research, lubricated with a generous digestif.

I soon learnt: Kilimanjaro is actually a dormant volcano which began forming approximately one million years ago and is part of a chain of volcanoes dotted along the East African Rift System. It last grumbled in anger around two hundred years ago, producing the familiar cone shape that we see today. In the middle of this cone is a crater called the Ash Pit, from within which sulphurous gases pervade the air - the classic eggy fart aroma. Here the ground is hot thus preventing ice from forming.

Rather than being part of a mountainous region or range, such as the Himalayas, Kilimanjaro proudly rises out of the dusty Tanzanian plains, approximately 200 miles south of the Equator, all by itself. It is famously the highest free-standing mountain in the world yet remarkably does not require any technical climbing skills to reach the top. Hence its huge appeal to inexperienced but eager and determined bumbling buffoons like myself.

I knew Kilimanjaro was 5,895 metres high but until I converted that into feet and inches, I hadn't appreciated what a big bugger it was. At 19,341 feet high it was in fact 17,947 feet higher than I'd ever stood before on foot. In metres, the difference was only 5,470 and therefore, on the face of it, appeared to be a pushover.

Obviously, I was aware that the challenge lay in Tanzania and therefore required a long-haul flight. However, I was ignorant of the fact that there was a choice of several routes up the mountain. I had naively presumed there was only one way up.

I sometimes despair at 'choice'. For instance, ordering a coffee used to be so simple: black/white, with/without? Then, 'cappuccino' arrived on the scene and I was just about OK with that as an option, especially as it was now possible to wear that stupid frothy moustache whilst drinking one. Always good for a cheap laugh if delivered with an oblivious deadpan face. Unlike my children, I never tire of this 'comedy gold' opportunity.

However, with the wide-spread arrival of coffee chains came far too many options for my liking: caffeinated, decaf, full, semi-skinned, soy, tall, small, latte, Americano, mocha, drink in, drink out, shake it all about… endless. The moment 'flat' and 'skinny' became puzzling questions way beyond the comprehension of this particular coffee-loving human bean, I moved to espresso. Single or double? Simple. Well, not exactly… No, I don't want water with it! Very occasionally, though, you are served an accompanying complimentary incisor-challenging hard brown Bakelite biscuit thingy. I don't mind those; they arrive with no questions asked.

I sometimes think the Communists have it sorted – Want a new suit? It comes in drab military grey. A new car is a drab blue Trabant, presumably with military grey trim and Chairman Mao Tse-tung's cracking, mandatory best-seller only comes in red.

Actually, to be fair, in the West, I don't seem to recall a choice of boiler suit colour at Guantanamo Bay.

In the UK we're very fortunate. The General Election provides a free choice between a party who will adopt short-term policies, ignore the poor and needy, and allow the privileged few to wallow in their greed, or a party who will adopt short-term policies, bankrupt the country, and allow the privileged few to wallow in their greed.

Russia though, provides three choices for their citizens: Putin, Prison or, as we've witnessed recently with utterly tragic consequences, Poisoning.

Anyway, I digress. I had to choose a route up the mountain.

Clearly, some follow-up research reading was required. And, if you're thinking of tackling Kilimanjaro there are two books which you must read: obviously this one but also *Kilimanjaro: The Trekking Guide to Africa's Highest Mountain* by Henry Stedman.

Being a bloke and therefore allergic to going shopping on the high street, I took to the Internet and ordered the latter from a retailer which is known to pay its full UK taxes.

Chapter 2 – Preparation

The book duly arrived. I voraciously consumed the contents. It quickly became quite apparent that Kilimanjaro (or "Kili" to those who have climbed it - incentive enough, surely?) was not simply a task involving buying some gear and putting a few preparatory training miles on the clock.

Henry's (I felt an instant connection with the amiable author) detailed guide had turned my 'casual project' into a far more complex undertaking. This naively unexpected turn of events prompted the purchase of a spiral-bound A5 notebook; I already possessed a pencil.

The notebook soon dropped onto the doormat. I was now ready to begin.

I'm a great advocate of lists. In fact, if I'm off to the corner shop and only require one item I still make a list. It's all too easy to walk into a retail environment and wonder why on Earth I am there. Under such circumstances, the bail-out option, if you'd prefer not to turn around and make an embarrassed exit, is to buy a newspaper. Perhaps, like me, you've even reached the classic stage in life of opening the fridge door and occasionally thinking, why?

And so, with great enthusiasm, the list began: the gear, the travel company and route up Kilimanjaro, the dates, the training plan, my Will (only slightly kidding), and worst of all, beyond any doubt whatsoever, the jabs.

One of Matt's middle names is 'The Great Outdoors'. As such, with the exception of a 5-Season sleeping bag, he had all the gear necessary for the trip. He didn't require a list.

As for myself, well, the only item of any use that I could immediately think of was a chunky chocolate bar. But, and to my credit, it was the variety that, supposedly, only "real men" can tackle, so it wasn't a bad start.

New Year's Day arrived together with my final proposed hangover for the next six months. It also heralded the start of the epoch of the metamorphosis from an ever so slightly, beginning-to-let-things-slip-a-little-bit, sedentary, happy in his comfort zone, lardy lounge lizard into a peak fitness, raring to go, truly ripped explorer for whom mountains would simply roll over and surrender themselves to upon seeing his muscular masculine majesty *merely* approaching base camp let alone embarking upon the final push to ultimate glory; I think it's important to have a modest vision.

My body was, on the verge of, setting off on the relentless road to becoming a temple at which I would soon be worshipping, lighting joss sticks for and making appropriate offerings to with due reverence. It would be a gruelling journey but I was prepared to uncompromisingly pander to its every requirement. As I perused the various trekking routes up Kilimanjaro a packet of crisps stared at me invitingly - "Eat me" it said - and I felt obliged to put it out of its misery. So I did.

On 2 January, I found some old hiking boots and delicately evicted the spiders that had set up an 'arachnosquat' inside. I packed a rucksack full of snacks and spare clothing before opening the front door and setting off on an adventurous four-mile walk. It was to be a local walk, sticking to pavements and well-trodden footpaths, and certainly not requiring a map. In fact, it wasn't at all 'adventurous' if I'm honest.

After a mile, I was craving a cup of tea so made a mental note to add a flask to my training kit list. An hour and a half later, I had successfully found my way home. OK, it was a modest start and my normally sedentary feet had blistered, but I felt really pleased with myself.

Remarkably, on another training hike, this time along the tranquil upper reaches of the River Thames, I spotted a moored boat. Its name was "Uhuru"! At 5,895 metres, the highest point on Kilimanjaro, and every trekker's ultimate goal, is called "Uhuru Peak". Being a naturally and, at times, stiflingly superstitious person (to the extent of having a rigidly set and largely unsuccessful routine involving choice of underwear, beverage consumption and, I kid you not, equating the numbers of cars I let out in front of me to goals scored, on the way up to The Hawthorns on match days), I took this as a good omen, a portentous sign of imminent success, especially as the boat appeared to be in good condition, barnacle-free and afloat; rather like myself.

The very top of Kilimanjaro had in actual fact, for many years, been referred to as "Kaiser Wilhelm Peak". It was so named by Hans Meyer, a German chap, who was the first known conqueror of this highest point on the African continent.

By the late nineteenth century, and with the British and Germans busying themselves in East Africa, there had been several failed attempts to reach the summit, largely due to altitude sickness and the thick ice sheets.

In 1887, and learning from the previous climbs of others, Meyer made his first ascent of the mountain. However, this expedition failed in much the same way as those before him. His return a year later coincided with the Abushiri Revolt - effectively an Arab uprising, led by Al Bashir ibn Salim al-Harthi, against the resident Germans and their East Africa Company. Meyer was captured and held hostage, eventually paying a huge ransom to Al Bashir for his release.

Undeterred, the German was back again a year later and finally summited on 6 October 1889. His account of the whole experience was published in 1890 (translated into, what I consider, classic Victorian explorer's English, in 1891) and titled *Across East African Glaciers*. Meyer's description of those final historic moments went as follows:

"I was the first to set foot on the culminating peak, which we reached at half-past ten o'clock. Taking out a small German flag, which I had brought with me for the purpose in my knapsack, I planted it on the weatherbeaten lava summit with three ringing cheers, and in virtue of my right as its first discoverer christened this hitherto unknown and unnamed mountain peak - the loftiest spot in Africa and in the German Empire - Kaiser Wilhelm's Peak. Then we gave three cheers more for the Emperor, and shook hands in mutual congratulation. Njaro, the

19

guardian spirit of the mountain, seemed to take his conquest with a good grace, for neither snow nor tempest marred our triumphal invasion of his sanctuary. The icefields flashed and glittered in the dazzling sunlight, the wind sighed whisperingly in the crannies and crevices, and in the depths of the yawning cauldron at our feet light wreaths of vapour curled softly and ceaselessly. For a few minutes we gave ourselves up to the impressive charm of our surroundings, and then suddenly awoke to the prosaic fact that it was long past breakfast-time, and that our inner man was becoming significantly conscious of 'a felt want.' Having deposited the topmost stone of the pile in my knapsack, we made our way back to the edge of the crater. Here we sat down, and after a hearty meal, proceeded to make a closer inspection of our surroundings."

Meyer, as you've just read, planted a German flag and named the summit after the Kaiser and then left his towel on a nearby pile of stones to bag his spot ready for his return very early the next morning (I have to admit that some of these comments are a very poor and lazy, outdated, stereotypical, un-PC joke about German holidaymakers for which I unreservedly apologise. Any complaints should be addressed to my Editor).

Meyer had summited along with Ludwig Purtscheller, an alpine expert from Salzburg, and Yohani Kinyala Lauwo (known as Kinyala), a local Chagga (a large ethnic group of the Kilimanjaro region) villager. It is, in my view, a similar story to that of Tenzing Norgay (the local Nepalese Sherpa) who, along with Edmund Hillary, were the first known climbers to summit Mount Everest/Chomolungma/Sagarmatha.

Only two months later, Al Bashir (who had held Meyer hostage) was himself captured, sentenced to death and hanged. Kinyala, however, would reportedly live to one hundred and twenty-five years old, become Kilimanjaro's most famous guide and astonishingly was present at the 1989 centennial celebrations of that first summiting!

Interestingly, some reports suggest that Kinyala may have summited Kilimanjaro on several occasions *before* the successful Meyer expedition; he should have left *his* towel at the top as proof. Again, parallels can be drawn with the intriguing George Mallory and Andrew Irvine conundrum - did they, didn't they, summit Everest in 1924, thirty years before Hillary and Norgay?

When Tanzania gained independence in 1961, part of the celebrations included the renaming of the summit to 'Uhuru Peak'. In Swahili, 'Uhuru' translates as 'Freedom'.

Anyway, back to *my* story now. After three weeks of bravely venturing out in Middle England's cosy shires' landscape on my own, I invested in my first ever smartphone. With the help of my son, I, ok, strictly speaking, he downloaded the 'Endomondo' app.

I'd heard the word 'app' on many occasions and completely ignored it, hoping it would go away, but now I'd got one! It was brilliant. I could track where I'd been, how far I'd walked and, in case of emergencies, my long-suffering and incredibly tolerant wife could always locate me or, indeed, ignore me - assuming I'd remembered to switch on the crucial 'Location' feature.

I'd also invested in some rather pricy hiking boots - well, 'buy cheap, buy twice' is so true - and a 35-litre rucksack. Though I say it myself, I was beginning to look the part. Things were getting serious.

In early February, I met up with Matt to walk the length of the Malvern Hills from south to north. The 'hills' are located approximately thirty-five miles south west of Birmingham, in the rural setting of Worcestershire. Featuring some of oldest rocks in England, they run almost exactly in a north-south direction for 10 miles or so. Due to their outstanding solitude, set within a relatively low-lying landscape, they appear as a long, slumbering dragon-like creature when viewed from afar and afford evocative panoramic views from the many peaks.

Malvern is, arguably, most famous for its uniquely pure water which, when walking the hills, is constantly free 'on tap' from the various springs dotted along their length.

However, in my experience, there is far more than water on offer: the hills, the air, the town and its hostelries are a perfect natural stimulant for thought-provocation and creativity. WH Auden, CS Lewis, JRR Tolkien, R Binout and Sir Edward Elgar, to name but a few of the greats in music and literature, have all found inspiration there.

It seems ridiculous to me now but back in February I had been rather apprehensive about this hike with Matt. I'd never attempted such a lengthy 'expedition' before.

We set off from the southern tip of the hills together and had agreed beforehand to push ourselves at our own pace otherwise Matt would have gained precious little benefit had he simply 'ambled' along with me. He was ever so slightly marginally far far fitter than me so his 'natural' pace was much faster than mine. As a consequence, we were soon separated; me panting and puffing at the rear but blissfully content whilst watching my companion glide effortlessly off into the distance.

Over the course of the day, this 'understanding' allowed Matt to enjoy several tea stops, turn around and admire the view of his red-faced buddy attempting to keep up.

However, I eventually discovered my own comfortable hiking pace. It was one which had arrested my concerning chest ache and shooting pains down my left arm, and by the time I arrived at the day's high point, the Worcestershire Beacon, some six and half miles after commencing, I felt genuinely elated. I was so pleased to see Matt again presuming he'd possibly arrived at the Beacon two days before me. Actually, and rather to my pleasantly satisfied amazement which I pretended to take very much in my stride, he was only fifteen minutes ahead. It was now one o'clock and time for lunch.

I'd been to the top of the Beacon many times before and, at 425 metres (1,394 feet), it was the highest I'd ever been on foot. It seemed daunting, as I absorbed the wonderful scenery that had been witnessed by so many before me, that this 'pimple' I was casually resting upon was merely **one fourteenth** of the height of Kilimanjaro. Crikey!

However, with little 'pomp and circumstance' I reached inside my rucksack, pulled out lunch and gazed across, in a westerly direction, to the mountains of South Wales... hmm? There were 'pimples' galore over there. More than could ever be found on a teenage boy's puberty-ravaged pizza face. Some big ones too.

Whilst triumphantly tucking into my sandwiches, I reminisced with Matt about the old wooden café that used to be situated only a few feet away from where we were currently sitting; a place which had been such a treat for me as a child. For climbing up to the top of the Beacon without having a tantrum, strop or other sproggly whinges, we would be rewarded for our saintly pilgrimage with that, in hindsight, worryingly thick sickly *Cresta – It's Frothy Man* sugary drink and an ice cream. If we were very good indeed, we'd be permitted a *Flake* in the ice cream too; a '99', I seem to recall.

Matt had discretely tuned-out my wittering but a lady nearby had overheard the one-sided conversation so together we proceeded to happily recall the old structure and generally chatted like two nostalgic geriatrics.

But Matt and I were on a mission and before a scene from the *Last of the Summer Wine* could fully develop, I bade goodbye to the old biddy and headed off on the final stretch of the hike.

After finishing, I excitedly found my phone and looked at the app readings: DISTANCE - 10.38 miles, DURATION - 4h:16m:11s. It had been nothing more than a leisurely stroll for Matt but, for me, it had been a worthy test both mentally and physically. It had also been an utterly revelatory window on a new world of getting out into the countryside.

I had previously considered that 'going out for a bit of walk' was the domain of old people who couldn't sit still on account of rheumatism or incontinence. I was wrong. *Anyone* could enjoy this. I was now hooked on hiking.

Since that day, I have notched up a few thousand miles in mountains, along ancient tracks and coastal footpaths, dense forests and jungles and, without exception, have benefited from every single outing. It has provided an opportunity to immerse myself in the meandering tangles of my thoughts, marvel at the varied beauty of our precious planet, strike up conversations with complete strangers and experience many spiritual moments. It is the perfect antidote and therapy for an always-connected, claustrophobic modern life. And, at the end of a particularly long hike, there is no better tiredness to induce a good night's sleep - perhaps I should add the caveat that it's a good night's sleep at what we might loosely refer to as sea level. Altitude, as I would discover, is the ultimate sleep-slayer.

I ventured out at every opportunity, making sure I was carrying six or seven kilos of clothing and provisions in my rucksack as this is what I would be carrying on Kilimanjaro.

The next big opportunity to venture out occurred on 29 April, when Kate and William were getting hitched so it was a public holiday.

I regard myself as a passive fan of the Royal Family and think, in every sense of the word, we're a richer country as a result of this heritage but I have no interest whatsoever in settling down to watch one of their weddings, nor anybody else's for that matter. In fact, during my own wedding, I had a hidden earpiece so that I could follow how Albion were getting on - only kidding... er... maybe. The match ended 2-2 by the way.

So, whilst preparations were being made for Royal Wedding street parties, I headed to South Wales and, in particular, the Brecon Beacons. I set off early, armed with my OS map folded open with a big yellow highlight marking the Lower Neuadd Reservoir. I'd planned, for me, a challenging route to encompass the peaks of Corn Du, Pen y Fan, Cribyn and Fan y Big.

There was the early shock of having to pay a toll to enter South Wales followed by a stressful drive to the reservoir. Yes, I was in possession of my new mobile phone but I hadn't yet discovered its sat nav capabilities and once I'd reached Merthyr Tydfil it was a nightmare to find the correct B-road. I'm a typical bloke. I simply refuse to ask for directions. Besides, I would have been far too embarrassed to display my ignorance at not being able to pronounce 'Neuadd'. Mind you, that paled into insignificance when looking at some of the features along my proposed hiking route: Twyn Mwyalchod, Graig Fan Ddu, Rhiw yr Ysgyfarnog and Bwlch Duwynt. Good luck with those! In fact, should you ever meet anyone who can pronounce and spell such words then you simply must grab them as a *Scrabble* partner.

At this point, I want to stress that whenever I've ventured abroad, I have always attempted to learn the absolute basics of 'hello', 'please' and 'thank you' in the local language. I take great pride in this and consider it to be the polite and correct thing to do. In fact, on a visit to a market in Borneo my attempt to say 'thank you' in Malay resulted in the warmest of smiles and biggest of hugs all round, or perhaps I'd just paid a ridiculous amount of money for a bracelet enabling the stall holder to retire.

Additionally, when subsequently hiking in Wales or Scotland I have endeavoured to learn how to pronounce the various peak names. One of my favourite hikes takes in Fan Brycheiniog and I was so pleased when I'd learnt how to reel off that name fluently. Sadly, only one person has ever heard me attempt to 'reel it off' though.

I did eventually find my way to the car park at the Neuadd (pronounced 'Nee ath' in case you were wondering) Reservoir and commenced the hike in thick mist.

The first part was a steep six hundred feet climb to a cairn followed by a reasonably level path heading north. After a further half-hour, the cloud broke and I realised I was looking down an almost sheer cliff face into the valley below. It was breath-takingly stunning and exhilarating in equal measure. I was feeling rather content and, also, knew exactly where I was on the OS map. Result!

I've always possessed a good sense of direction and could map-read at an early age so it shouldn't have come as a complete surprise. Nevertheless, to know where you are in an exposed and unfamiliar environment was encouraging, so much so that I stopped, opened up my flask of tea and toasted my map-reading skills. I sipped at the steaming brew drinking in the beautiful yet unpronounceable landscape.

With a quenched thirst and glowing vigour, I set off towards the peak of Corn Du. I was, sensibly, carrying a rucksack full of fleecy layers, gloves, a hat, full waterproofs, food, drink, map and compass and first-aid kit so it came as a huge shock when a couple came ambling towards me wearing plimsolls, seemingly only a couple of layers of clothing and carrying a small canvas bag between them.

They stopped and asked me for directions to the footpath which would take them down to the car park. I was uncertain of the greater surprise: that they were so inadequately clothed or the fact that they were asking *me*, a total newcomer, for directions.

To them I obviously looked like a seasoned hiker so, playing along with my new role as 'park ranger' and totally basking in the unwarranted glory, I suavely produced my map and spread it out over a nearby outcrop of rocks. Unfortunately for me, a gust of wind blew it from my grasp forcing me to chase after it like a child trying to catch a jumping frog. I was thoroughly disappointed with the way my charade was quickly fading.

However, the second attempt was a major triumph. Map flat, I pointed out our position, informing the casual walkers that they'd come too far and should retrace their footsteps for approximately 400 yards and then turn south west - I could have said 'left' but I was showing off now - at the junction of footpaths.

I made sure not to attempt mentioning any of the place names on the map just in case it blew my cover. I even offered that they would be more than welcome to join me as I was heading their way. However, they were happy simply with my instructions and sat down to enjoy a *Mars* bar each.

Thankfully the potentially awkward re-folding of the billowing map went like a treat. I set off again with a huge sense of pride and community spirit, and then almost immediately tripped on a rock. Naturally, I attempted to turn the stumble into a classic 'I meant to do that' moment and carried on as though nothing untoward had happened. Another classic, the old 'throw them off the scent with casual whistling', may have attracted unnecessary attention so I kept quiet. I didn't dare turn around. I'll never know whether they noticed. Hopefully the challenge of the chewy caramel and chocolate bar had them otherwise occupied.

Upon reaching the top of Corn Du, I once again referred to the map. I was eager to learn how high I was and if truth be told, I was totally out of breath; a fact perfectly disguised to any onlookers by pretending to immerse myself in some, apparently, most important 'map research'. At 873 metres it was, by some distance, the highest I'd ever been on foot.

Pen y Fan, to the east, was next and, being only a short walk away, I set off with great anticipation.

Only ten minutes later I was standing and panting breathlessly at the highest point in the whole of South Wales. What a wonderful sense of achievement for this mountain novice. I absorbed the panorama and nodded and smiled benevolently to the others who'd also reached the flat, rocky summit.

At 886 metres this was now the highest I'd ever been on foot. Despite my personal sense of achievement, it was slightly annoying that, when measured in feet, I'd not quite reached 3,000; it was in fact 2,907. Little did I know that, in a few weeks' time, simply by standing on the tarmac at Kilimanjaro International Airport, I would break my record and find myself at an elevation of 894 metres. At 2,933 feet it would still be, annoyingly, below the 3,000 mark though.

I began to feel a slight chill and so descended, in an easterly direction, along Craig Cwm Sere for a much-deserved lunch break. Being clothed appropriately, sitting down enjoying sandwiches, snacks and a flask of tea whilst admiring a spectacular view is certainly one of life's treasured moments. No artificial distractions. Just me and the mountains. It was intoxicating. Rather like my sandwich, as it turned out, which had far too much mustard in it. It made me smile though. What a superfluous problem to have in this rustic dining room of tranquillity.

Continuing towards the east, Cribyn was the next high point, followed by a steep descent and an equally strenuous climb up to the final peak of the day, Fan y Big.

I am fully aware that 'F' is pronounced as a 'V' in Welsh but, nevertheless, the name of this particular feature will always conjure up images, in my mind, of a generously proportioned past girlfriend, 'Mad Mandy'. Yes, I know, that's all very schoolboyish but Bon Scott didn't do too badly with the similarly shaped 'Whole Lotta Rosie': "She ain't exactly pretty, Ain't exactly small, 42-39-56, You could say she's got it all."

Fan y Big – getting to the summit turned out, in fact, to be a 'Whole Lotta struggle' to 'bag' as my inexperienced legs and lungs failed to function as they had done so admirably earlier in the day. However, the afternoon fatigue was fairly easy enough to shrug off as I reminded myself it was an excellent workout for what lay ahead in Africa.

Once back at Neuadd, I checked my mobile phone eagerly noting the stats: DISTANCE - 9.86 miles, DURATION - 4h:20m:36s, and CALORIES - 1,064 kcal, which I swiftly converted into 3 pints or a bottle of wine.

Returning home in the car, I was pleasantly surprised to discover that there was no toll to return to England. That was equivalent to another bottle of wine!

Three weeks later, I was back in the Brecons for a particularly gruelling hike. This time with Matt. Another middle name of his is 'Got all the gear' and of particular interest to me were his lightweight waterproof trousers which were significantly lighter and more practical than my golfing ones which I'd thus far been wearing for my hikes. I wasn't planning on taking my clubs up Kilimanjaro so had been looking into the value of purchasing good quality lightweight trouser attire for the trip instead of wearing my golfing ones.

Following two hours of surreptitious admiration, I took a couple of photos of Matt wearing his impressive trousers, with the intention of 'accidentally unknowingly' purchasing an identical pair once home... what a complete coincidence that would be! Matt's suspicions were aroused, though, when it was all too obvious that I was only focusing my camera on his waist downwards. So, swallowing my copycat pride, it was far simpler and much less awkward just to fess up and ask him for the brand details. Without wanting to advertise, unless sponsored (take note, *erghaus), all I'll say is that the brand name began with 'B' and they were a worthy purchase.

Our route was similar to the one I had followed on my previous solo visit. However, on this particular hike, upon pausing at the top of Cribyn, we decided to go 'off-piste' - for a laugh, as chaps do. Well, the weather was set fair, we were in high spirits and we had all day.

Rather than taking the established path to the south and east, we headed north east along a steep descending route, annotated on the map as Bryn Teg. After ten minutes, we turned due east, off the path, and stumbled down into a steep valley full of lush, thick grass of calf muscle height with the odd hawthorn bush punctuating the landscape.

By the time we reached a small stream at the bottom, Cribyn was towering thirteen hundred feet above us. It appeared mightily impressive in its unattainability.

We were now stood somewhere near to, or in, Cwm Cynwyn. That was, though, largely irrelevant for, to reach 'Mandy's Big Fan y', or whatever it was called, we'd now left ourselves a challenging, vertiginous scramble of a thousand feet. Upwards. Well yes, we had all day, I supposed again, despite beginning to curse and question our decision not to follow the, now, way more appealing dotted green line on the OS map.

Half way up our impromptu 'slope to freedom', we called a team meeting and stopped for a cup of tea. Amidst much panting and swearing, we began to hesitantly joke about the audacious challenge we'd set ourselves by going 'off-piste for a laugh'.

I would later discover that being able to laugh in the ugly, taunting face of high-altitude despair was an essential attribute for staying positive.

I reminded myself that this latest struggle would benefit my fitness levels and increase my mental stamina. After all, it was rapidly becoming oh so clear to me that on Kilimanjaro the mental side of the challenge was at least equal to the physical one.

Whilst regaining my breath, Matt and I explored the old chestnut of why the local sheep had evolved shorter left legs than their right ones, resulting in effortless anticlockwise grazing of the grass. The only disadvantage to this Darwinian step that we could see was that if a sheep turned around, maybe to revisit a particularly delicious tuft of vegetation, it would inevitably tumble down the valley to a boggy fate. Or, if a randy ram ever found himself in front of a potential mate then he would have to wander all the way round the mountain in order to get into the entry position again. Well, it made us laugh at the time.

It was, of course, all very light-hearted but I did then, in a testing-the-water sort of way, express my 'slight' concerns over the forthcoming trip and the fact that here I was finding *only* a Welsh mountain quite a struggle.

I didn't really need to explain any further for Matt knew what was looming in the back of my mind. He turned around to face me properly and promised that he would be staying right by my side on Summit Day. He would get me to the top of Kilimanjaro.

Yes, we were still being quite jovial but I appreciated that, in the under-current of my testing of the water, Matt had just made a solemn commitment. That one declaration would stay with me every single day throughout our eventual trip in faraway Tanzania. Matt *would* get me to the top; wouldn't he?

We pressed on, no footpath to follow, staggering in a mostly upwards direction until, finally, I'd never been more relieved to see Fan y. It was an exhilarating climax and warranted yet another cup of tea before the afterglow of the much less brutal descent back to the car.

At the end of this particular outing our stats were: DISTANCE - 11.12 miles, DURATION - 5h:21m:06s, CALORIES - 1,201 kcal (another chilled bottle of Gavi *plus*, this time, a generous chunk of Cheddar), and our overall total accumulated ascent was 3,577 feet. I was shattered. As Tommy Cooper would have said, "I slept like a log last night, woke up in the fireplace."

Without wanting to sound like an advert for the Wales Tourist Board, I've pretty much trekked all over the Brecons now. I never tire of the magnificence of the scenery and return as often as possible.

Subsequently, my post-Kilimanjaro trekking travels then took me further north to Snowdonia where the landscape is, arguably, even more dramatic and with the exception of Snowdon itself, it's very easy to find wonderful isolation.

When attempting to encapsulate the effect this part of the world might have on oneself, I always consider the progression of Led Zeppelin's first three albums: two opening stonking, blues-based rock albums; the band, next, retreating to the isolated cottage of Bron Yr Aur in Snowdonia; then emerging like a butterfly from a chrysalis with the release of a largely folk-based rock album of *Led Zeppelin III*. It's fair to say that this album wasn't everyone's cup of tea but I certainly enjoyed the acoustic brew in the vinyl vessel that featured many classic tracks.

Like a great deal of acoustic folk-rock music, at times, I find Snowdonia a capricious medley of fiddles, guitars, mandolins, flutes, harps, whistles and, if I could find someone to play it, I would also throw in an occasional hurdy-gurdy too.

Since venturing to Tanzania and many other destinations around the world, I have begun to fully appreciate that the UK is blessed with an extremely varied and historic landscape, all contained within a relatively small area: mountains, coasts, moorlands and wilderness, plus many stunning National Parks too. There are numerous ancient tracks and landscapes which can awaken our inner ancestors and, to me at least, bristle with the spirituality and wisdom of our past. And, very occasionally, the sun shines too but, as of yet, I've never bumped into the fabled "Walking Man's Crumpet".

On one of my trips abroad, I met a Canadian who remarked upon, with great envy, the UK's network of public footpaths and 'right to roam', ending by saying that one might be shot at by a banjo-bearing 'local' in North America if caught wandering around in the countryside. He also mentioned, 'squealing like a pig', at which point I put my fingers in my ears. Our, perhaps, equally-taken-for-granted NHS is also frequently admiringly commented upon during my travels. Travel is unquestionably enlightening.

Chapter 3 – The dreaded part

The physical and, inadvertently, the mental side of preparation was going really well. I felt fitter than at any stage since the age of thirteen. Up until then I'd played for the school football team being a highly proficient 'utility' (a kind way of describing someone who was rubbish at every position on the pitch) player at right-back, right-half and, my favourite: inside-right. You may be surprised to learn that I preferred my right foot.

I only scored one solitary goal during my school days but I can remember it ever so clearly, even today - a turn, a short dribble a powerful run followed by an unstoppable rocket of a, yes, right-footed piledriver into the top of the goal. (Incidentally, a few years later, Cyrille Regis copied my move and won BBC's *Match of the Day's* Goal of the Season. Whilst Cyrille's fine effort is on YouTube, mine isn't.) I should place my moment of glory into some form of context by admitting that my goal came in a 12-0 victory over embarrassingly inferior opposition when even our inert, colossus lump of a centre-half ('Porky' Porter) managed to score that day.

I was devastated when, upon moving up to the senior school, football was dropped and we played two terms of rugby. I absolutely love rugby today but back then I despised it with a passion. Up until that point, with my slight, Lionel Messi-like build (but that's most certainly where any comparisons ended), I'd shone over the larger kids at football but now these "colossus lumps", including 'Porky', were far superior in the physical, grubby underworld of the rugby tackles and scrums. I very quickly worked out that scrum-half or preferably the wing, were the ideal or, should I admit, 'safest' positions for me.

Every school year I consequently longed for the summer term of cricket. At junior school this sport had not endeared itself to me even though, like rugby and football, I follow it avidly today. The problem initially was the shared school kit; everything was far too big. I was a slightly better-than-average wicket-keeper but the gloves were far too big and would all too easily fly off my hands when returning the ball to the bowler.

And there would always be stagnant pools of sweat residing in the bottom of each glove finger kindly deposited there by the previous occupant.

Batting was even worse. I found it impossible to run normally, looking instead like a startled bow-legged chicken with thrush. The pads flapped like elephant ears, the buckles shredded the insides of my legs and simply holding the bat, let alone playing a stroke, with over-sized green spiky batting gloves was a challenge in itself.

The worst, of course, was the shared 'box' - the legendary piece of cricket equipment worn to protect the vulnerable delicate male, middle stump genitalia region which, as I was later informed by a jovial shop assistant, is never offered in a 'small' size.

The box always lurked menacingly at the bottom of the kit bag. The odour of the leather kit bag was dreadful enough but the box was from a murky sporting arena of sweaty glandular horrors. It certainly didn't encourage hanging about at the crease for a long innings. Personal hygiene simply did not register with young boys so there was always a lingering fear of contracting something unsavoury. There was even a rumour that one might catch 'VD' from the box. No one knew exactly what this 'VD' was but it did sound, potentially, quite nasty and was probably best avoided. Enough said.

By the time I was in the senior school, the cricket equipment all fitted perfectly and I absolutely loved playing our summer game both as a wicket-keeper and a very late-order, right-handed (what else) nurdler of a batsman. I'd even bought my own box (size medium, since you ask), etched my initials onto it and never once allowed anyone to borrow it, ever. I did catch VD though.

The logistical planning of the trip to Africa was hardly physically demanding, simply involving a great deal of online research, diligent referral to Henry's book, and chatting on the phone to Matt.

However, I hadn't anticipated the vast array of travel companies offering their services nor the matter of six routes up the mountain to choose from.

Also, I soon discovered that Mount Kilimanjaro actually has three summits; these three volcanic features are known as Kibo, Mawenzi, and Shira. Uhuru Peak is at the top of Kibo.

There was a huge range and variety of figures to mull over. Travel companies, for example, were very keen to boast high summit success rates, a large proportion of which were in the ninetieth percentiles.

Interestingly, when reading reports from sources without a vested interest in selling a trip, those figures tumbled to between 60 and 85%.

It was then quite easy to be slightly distracted by reports of 'occasional' fatalities. The official keeper of such records is the Kilimanjaro National Park (KINAPA) but they seem reluctant to publish the statistics. From my own research, I have estimated the number of deaths of climbers is in the region of one person every two months along with a similar number of guides and porters.

It appeared that approximately 50,000 people attempt Kilimanjaro every year with just under a quarter of those coming from the United States. The second highest nation represented is the UK, with a figure of half that of the US. It's worth bearing in mind, though, that UK's population is around a fifth of their cousins from across the Atlantic. Next on this list come the Germans followed by the Australians.

By my calculations, assuming a success rate of 80%, 40,000 climbers stand at Uhuru Peak each year, which equates to around 110 on an average day; is there such a thing as an average day on 'Kili', I wondered?

I became slightly side-tracked by reading all about the various records. To tackle Kilimanjaro, one is expected to be fit and must be above 10 years of age. So, the first record came as a bit of surprise when I discovered that the youngest person to summit 'Kili' was aged seven.

Conversely the oldest was 88 - something I might contemplate challenging during my retirement years... but then again, maybe not.

The various routes up to the top generally take hikers five or six days and that gave me a guideline with which to consider what the fastest time might be... but, come on! Swiss mountain runner Karl Egloff ran to the top in 4 hours and 56 minutes and completed the whole ascent and descent in 'only' a credulity-stretching 6 hours 42 minutes. Really? (Source: www.climbmountkilimanjaro.com).

These records all sounded ridiculous when reading them pre-trip. Post-trip, they became totally outrageously ridiculous!

Anyway, it was quickly apparent that the longer the number of days spent climbing on the ascent had a direct correlation with the summiting success rate, simply because the body was given more time to acclimatise. As such, we chose the route that offered the greatest number of ascent days: the Lemosho Route.

Interestingly, the British Mountaineering Council (BMC), on their website (www.thebmc.co.uk), offer plenty of advice on recommended rates of ascent. One article states that above 3,000 metres (possibly even 2,500) an increase in 300 metres in sleeping altitude per day is the best practice for a healthy adult. So, using this guideline, an ascent from 3,000 to 6,000 metres (which is extremely similar to a Kilimanjaro climb) should take 10 days.

The Lemosho Route provided us with six days of ascent to reach the final 'base camp', as opposed to the five the other routes, at that time, offered before the final summit-night push to Uhuru Peak. As a consequence, the trip was more expensive but our main consideration was to maximise our chances of reaching the summit in what we viewed as a once-in-a-lifetime opportunity.

This particular route also appeared to be more remote, less busy in the early stages and was the most varied in terms of landscape and vegetation. In all, its total length was approximately 70km (43½ miles).

I then had to check that the trip was running within given time parameters: it couldn't commence before the end of the football season and I had to be back home before the schools broke up for the summer holidays. Albion's final game of the season was on 22 May and the schools broke up mid-July. At the time of planning the trip, the Baggies had relegation concerns so it was *even* more important for me to attend the games, offer my support, and somehow affect results.

Many years ago, my obsession with not missing home games led to a seemingly extraordinary decision. It was November 1993 and I was a video Buyer for a major UK retailer. Cindy Crawford, the supermodel, was flying over to the UK on a three-day whirlwind tour to promote her latest fitness video and I was invited to attend its launch party at a plush London hotel. Representing the high street's market-leader in the sales of Health & Fitness for 'Home Videos', I was going to be seated next to Cindy for the evening meal.

As I excitedly planned my underwear (or would I 'go commando'?) and what I might say to her, I casually checked my football fixtures diary. Would you believe it, the Albion were at home to Padova in the tin pot Anglo-Italian Cup tournament on the very same evening. A competition which was partly designed to forge harmonious international relationships but one which had the complete opposite effect with bad-tempered games, one-eyed referees and players fighting amongst themselves the norm. However, I hadn't missed a home game since the Coronation. But I couldn't let Cindy down, could I?

Of course, there was no decision to be made. I simply had to follow my ridiculously blind loyalty to the cause; one which is rarely rewarded. So, I was one of the 2,745 foolhardy souls who attended that match. A 3-4 defeat to boot! Defeats hit me badly but I also had a feeling of guilt that Cindy was even more distraught at having missed out on my company. She did send me a signed photo a few days later, which I still lovingly possess, but has never written to me since. I suppose I should let that one go.

Fortunately, Matt and I found a trip which suited us both. I booked it. That was that. We were now committed. Gulp! 'Chickening out' was not covered in the travel insurance small print.

So, apart from the snacks and medical necessities, my kit list had all been purchased, ticked and checked, the route, dates and travel company chosen, the flights booked and I had reached a level of mountain fitness that I was delighted with. In fact, I'd clocked-up just over two hundred miles of hiking in England and Wales during that five-month training period.

That left just one more major task on my 'things to do' list to tick off. More than anything else this, for me, was the dreaded one. Ever since finally deciding to tackle Kilimanjaro this was the one that had kept me awake at night. I would have to pull myself together, sweep aside the curtains of procrastination and front-up to the inexorable reality of the jabs!

During my life I've broken fingers and ribs, suffered many bloody cuts and wounds, caught my manly part in a zip, endured an endoscopy, passed a kidney stone (gosh, that really, really hurts!), and was even persuaded by a friend to watch his beloved Wolverhampton Wanderers attempt to play football once, but nothing fills me with more dread than needles. Needless to say, I entered my local surgery with absolute dread, cold clammy hands and overwhelming undiluted fear. I've even come out in a sweat now simply by writing about it. Had there been a wild animal in that waiting room it would surely have sensed my terrified state, taken full advantage, and devoured me. I would have been an easy kill. Fortunately, the room was only full of nearly-dead old people, so I was safe.

I'm sure this genuine phobia all began aged nine-years-old when we had a brutal, mass flu-jabbing at school. It was to be my one and only influenza inoculation for I pleaded with my folks, on bended knee and with no shortage of tears, never ever to return the parental permission form to school ever ever again. Even if they had, I would have found a way to intercept and destroy it.

And so, it was on a mid-morning Autumn day that our class queued in the hall to be 'shot'. Up the steps, onto the stage and then, with a spud-gun-like noise, what felt like a heavy lead weight was ruthlessly, brutally fired into my arm. Point blank range. As I gazed for the steps down off the raised platform, the hall span around and I collapsed into the mightily comforting bosom of Mrs Bailey.

I came to my senses in the school Sick Bay and was presented with a delicious bowl of chicken soup and accompanying bread roll. It's interesting to consider how much things change, especially technology. Back then, we didn't have a telephone at home so I spent the afternoon at school until it was time to catch the train home, being ever so careful to protect my butchered arm. A phobia was born!

The dentist soon also became associated with needles. It wasn't too long after 'Arm-ageddon' when I made a further association between fillings accompanied by torturous gum injections and sweets and fizzy drinks; completely giving up the tooth-rotting 'treats' in an instant.

Before I'd sussed this out, however, during one procedure, the anaesthetic hadn't fully taken effect and 'Butcher Wallace', the dentist, approached me again with yet another dose of 'numbing' fluid in a fearfully looming syringe with a needle the length of his arm. The 'poison' dripped out of its glistening tip. 'Butcher' had a sinister grin and laughed in my face with a, 'wah hah hah'. In a fit of tears and an instinctive act of self-preservation, I swiped his hand away. The 'weapon' fell to the floor.

After a brief, awkward moment of silence - surely this *had* happened before - I recall a slightly heated discussion involving the 'Butcher', his nurse, the voluptuous Ms Baker, and my Mum. The candlestick maker, like my now clearly delirious self, remained silent. There followed a rushed, brutal filling procedure, without the additional dose of anaesthetic, presumably containing a near-toxic quantity of mercury, hurriedly jammed into my sorry tooth.

I thought the 'episode' had ended reasonably well for all concerned but I just knew I'd be in trouble. Sure enough, in the car on the way home, my Mum gave me a right telling-off for my embarrassing behaviour. With my mouth deadened with numbness and one cheek feeling like a balloon I simply took it on the (numb) chin and said nothing.

That night the episode was retold to my Dad, in front of me, at which point Mum declared that she would never take me to the dentist's ever again. Did she mean that as a punishment? I desperately tried to hide my elation yet pretended to be severely chastised.

I tentatively returned to a 'friendly' dentist some twenty-seven years later in a brave act to set a good example to my children. Incredibly, and annoyingly for some, all that was required was a thorough clean. Mind you, by that time, I only possessed four yellow teeth. I now go every six months. Turned out alright in the end.

One incident which remains a source of irritation to this day was a hay fever jab administered on the sly. When I was fourteen years-old, my Mum, yep her again, took me to the doctor's. I had no idea what for, until it was too late. Nothing was mentioned. I was immersed in my teenage dream world, mostly involving *Pan's People*, while the adults conferred.

Then, without warning or provocation, the doctor savagely stabbed me. The room spun and I was caught by the barbaric perpetrator - where was the soft, accommodating Mrs Bailey?

That was the one and only time I suffered a hay fever jab. After that, I dosed-up on *Piriton* every year but in hindsight it now explains why, occasionally, I could barely stay awake in class let alone during the summer exams, which I now firmly believe accounts for my somewhat average 'O' and 'A' levels. I may still challenge the exam boards about my results.

Back at the local surgery, memories of 'bad jabs, gone bad' still at the forefront of my mind, my name flashed up on the screen and I was summoned to face the ordeal. Fortunately, the nurse was a very good friend so I'd felt comfortable in pre-warning her, on countless occasions, to the point of rolling-eyes boredom, about my fear of needles.

In Benny Hill fashion, I ran around the surgery at least four times before the nurse eventually collared me. I was then permitted to lie down for my 'major operation'.

I was pierced and poisoned with Typhoid, Hepatitis A, Tetanus, Diphtheria, Polio and Yellow Fever jabs in three separate assaults involving both my arms.

Admittedly, I hummed randomly during the procedure in a gamely attempt to distract myself from the shock and imminent pain but, I have to concede, the invasive procedure wasn't at all bad; I think today's instruments must be significantly thinner than the rusty old sewing needles from the dark ages of medical science used in the 1960s and 70s.

I was thrilled, totally surprised to find myself still conscious and only feeling mildly dizzy. A request for a cup of tea and a digestive biscuit was, disappointingly, a step too far. Maybe I should have gone 'private'?

So, I limped, yes limped, out of the abattoir. It had been one final pathetic attempt for sympathy and a sweet titbit; it had failed miserably.

However, once out of the surgery and into the open air, I actually felt rather ok and, of course, mightily relieved that the torment was finally over. I returned home, made my own cup of tea and treated myself to a 'medicinal' chocolate biscuit. The biggest pre-trip hurdle had been cleared with the absolute minimum of fuss.

By now, word of my trip was getting around and I was asked on several occasions whether I was doing it for charity. I wasn't. Charity events used to be a rarity. Now, every week seemingly, someone is doing

41

something for one charitable cause or another. I do, of course, appreciate that it's all extremely worthy and some wonderful causes are supported. I personally just feel a little uncomfortable when asking others for money. I didn't want to burden friends with yet another charity request. Besides, climbing Kilimanjaro was a very personal challenge and ambition, something which was hopefully going to reward and fulfil *me*.

I then completely changed my mind!

I decided to dedicate my trip to raising funds for the local primary school which was a friendly and vibrant presence in the centre of our small, rural village community. I had two children attending it and had discovered that our school, like all others, derived a significant income through the work of parents who organised fetes, coffee mornings and the like.

As usual, it was the good honest decent folk who rallied around; more than can be said about those obscene tax-avoiding online retail and social media giants, some of whom regard themselves as above the law, unaccountable and untouchable – grrrh!

Anyway, money raised for our school would be used to help fund school trips, laptops etc. I decided that for this cause, I felt comfortable with asking for donations.

So, it was accordingly announced in the school newsletter. As one thing led to another, I was invited to give a talk to the Year 3 class on the subject of mountains. It was a topic they were covering and I possibly presented an ideal opportunity to give an extracurricular and, hopefully, interesting account of my forthcoming expedition to them.

At the back of my mind I also considered that it would have been a tad awkward for the school to have asked me to talk to the kids, post-trip, in the event of me not summiting. Plus, it would have been completely impossible had I died in my attempt. So, fair play to school; excellent forward thinking.

I had plenty of research already collated, my agent squeezed a fee of £50,000 out of the poor school, so I gladly accepted the invitation to talk.

Apart from my daughter being squirmingly embarrassed at having her Dad in her class, the presentation went well with plenty of inquisitive questions being asked by young, enthusiastic minds.

It was also wonderful to see a smiling Danny in class. He was currently going through chemotherapy and only attended school whenever he was well enough to.

For all of us parents, it had been a numbingly, heart-stopping shock, striking at everyone's very core, when we'd first heard the news of his diagnosis of cancer. Goodness only knows what it must have been like for his parents! There seems to be something especially cruel when a child is diagnosed with cancer, so unfair.

A few days later, during the school run, Danny, with one of his bright-eyed, highly infectious trademark smiles, greeted me with, "Hello Mr Mountain Man." I smiled back at him. I could quite easily have cried though.

Chapter 4 – Africa here we come

One lovely June day, Matt arrived at my house. It wasn't too long before we'd spread out our equipment in order to make comparisons, as chaps do.

We'd prepared kit lists galore, shared many ideas about what to take during our training hikes and had engaged in several detailed phone calls over the past few weeks. Now was the chance for one final check before heading off to Heathrow.

Happy with our bags, Matt suddenly thought it would be a good idea to weigh them. It sounded eminently sensible to me and I fetched the bathroom scales. It hadn't occurred to us that we might be overweight but we were. So, after careful consideration and ranking items in order of importance, we removed a large quantity of energy gels and peanuts then came up with a brilliant idea to wear our heavy hiking boots for the flight. It worked a treat.

I always get slightly anxious at airport security. I'm not sure why. I've never attempted smuggling anything untoward but I always feel guilty. My face must portray criminal intent because, whether the scanner beeps or not when I pass through, I am usually stopped for a search.

At Heathrow, it was therefore of no real surprise when I set the alarm off and was thoroughly searched by someone with a character bypass whom I thought I recognised as a member of 'Spectre' in the *From Russia with Love* Bond film.

However, I do fully appreciate the current security concerns, whole-heartedly support it and recognise that this is not a procedure that is improved by inappropriate flippant comments from passengers. Safety first is paramount. Even though I was permitted through, I still sensed that at any moment a foreboding hand would be placed firmly on my shoulder and I'd be led off for interrogation and an 'internal'.

It was at this point that I discovered I was struggling to read the various travel documents I'd printed off. I was clearly, or unclearly, slightly long-sighted when wearing my contact lenses which I wore to correct my short-sightedness. So, we headed off to a certain retailer - without wanting to advertise, unless sponsored (take note, *oots the Chemist*), all I'll say is that they begin with 'B' - to purchase a pair of reading spectacles. Without my contact lenses in, I could read books and paperwork perfectly but then required glasses for distance. All part of the aging process I surmised.

As we walked past the travel adaptors we looked at one other quizzically and fashioned a raised eyebrow each. Onlookers would surely have considered us as two members of the Great Britain & Ireland Synchronised Eyebrow Raising team. Tanzania? Africa? Hmm? So, we bought a couple of adaptors just in case.

As a special treat, I'd booked us access to an airport lounge at Heathrow much to Matt's surprise and delight. Neither of us had experienced this luxury before but it seemed like an ideal way with which to begin our special adventure.

Whilst tucking into the free delicious food, at the 4 Deck Executive Lounge (they don't sponsor me either), Matt, to my great surprise, revealed yet another middle name, that of 'I'm ever so slightly very scared of flying'. Blimey, he might as well have ripped my shirt off, tweaked my nipples and called me Gladys.

Once the shock had subsided, I arrived at the perfect solution, presenting him with a generous-sized gin and tonic. It was just the tonic, in fact. I personally never drink alcohol on flights but this seemed appropriate for the situation. A subsequent follow-up 'settler' did just that.

The flight, of course, was long, tedious, fidget-inducing and quality sleep was not really feasible. Little had I realised that the previous night's sleep at home would be the last proper one for well over a week. After leaving Heathrow at 20:30, we arrived in Nairobi at 06:30 the following day. There was very little time to do anything other than take some paracetamol for a nasty headache and locate our next flight.

On arriving at Gate 3, 'Matt The Disorganised' discovered that he'd lost his boarding pass. Fortunately, it didn't seem to matter; he was permitted to climb onto the shuttle bus for the short ride to our propeller-propelled plane. It took off at 08:15 and by 09:00 we'd arrived at Kilimanjaro airport where, having stepped down out of the plane and without realising it, I was standing at the highest point on Earth I'd ever been on foot before.

This final flight had been fairly unspectacular, that is, with the exception of catching our first glimpse of the challenge that lay ahead. Out of a left-hand window, the top of Kilimanjaro revealed itself above the cloud line. It appeared both spectacular and menacing and, due to only being able to view the top one thousand metres or so, it was difficult to perceive the challenge as a whole. Instead, I found comfort in taking some snaps and pretending not to be utterly overwhelmed and a tiny bit terrified.

I do find airports confusing and stressful. It was therefore a relief that this was our final pass through customs and all the associated checks. I had predicted the Yellow Fever certificate requirement as well as form-filling. I hadn't expected to have a fingerprint taken though but simply adhered to any request. I was, after all, totally innocent of any crime. Again, to my guilt-ridden relief, no hand was slapped on my shoulder to whisk me away for another 'internal'. We then searched for our hold bags which thankfully arrived with very little delay.

Soon, we were able to stroll out of the airport and into the humidity of Tanzania. We'd made it. How wonderful it felt, all mixed with a tingling sense of adrenalised anticipation.

I saw a small group of travellers standing next to branded kit bags and realised they were part of our group for the next few days. We walked over to them.

I really do enjoy meeting new people, hearing their stories and trying to gain an early insight into whether each individual might be good fun, interesting to talk to or possibly one to avoid.

What I absolutely dread and fear is the 'remembering the names game'. I've tried every tactic in the manual, including the obvious one of repeating the name instantly and then blatantly inserting it into the conversation at the earliest opportunity. It simply does not work for me. In this aspect, Matt and myself were hopeless equals and therefore were perpetually and surreptitiously comparing notes on who was called what.

On approaching the group, I quickly evaluated the 'competition' and gravitated straight to the oldest-looking and, to put it bluntly, largest-around-the-middle participant. Dougie announced his name and in a flash of inspiration my panicking mind informed me he was 'Doughnut Dougie'. Brilliant! And, so long as I remembered to never, ever use the associated adjective in an audible sense, I couldn't fail to forget Dougie's name nor, for that matter, insult him.

I unearthed that Doughnut, sorry, I mean Dougie, was sixty-four years-old, and by the sound of his accent was from the North East of England. Despite having calf muscles the size of tree trunks, it was patently obvious that the majority of the remainder of his body had seen better days. I felt comforted simply by standing next to him; for possibly an awkwardly longer time than I should have, if truth be told. By comparison, he was making me look trim and ever so fit. I knew I would never beat him in a drinking race but I'd surely be faster up a mountain. Not that it's a race I reminded myself. Little snippets of Henry's book were engraved into my head and one piece of absolutely crucial advice is just that: 'Slowly, slowly' or 'Pole, Pole' (the 'e' pronounced as an 'ay' sound) as they say in Swahili. This, Henry insisted, was paramount to the success of the climb. But hopefully I could 'Pole, Pole' faster than Dougie.

I then recalled other vital information, such as: drink 4-5 litres of water each day, ensure you experience perpetual and clear peeing, adopt a positive mental attitude, listen to your guides at ALL times, and fart a lot - "if you're farting well, you're faring well" - too true as it turned out. I was so pleased with myself for having undertaken all that pre-trip research and being armed with all the necessary secrets to a successful summit... consequently, it should be a walk in the (Kilimanjaro National) park, right?

In an attempt to extend my conversation with Dougie, I asked whether he supported Newcastle or Sunderland and was flabbergasted to discover that he didn't follow football! There was a subsequent slightly awkward silence as we searched for common ground.

So, with my face possibly betraying a look of shock, I decided to pester someone else. It was a shame really because I'd recently heard what I considered to be a really good, North East regional-relevant joke and would have used it there and then as an ice-breaker. Oh well, maybe later.

Matt and I sidled over to four other members of the group, introduced ourselves and then attempted to pin their names into our memories. I think, between the two of us, we were only certain of a chap named Steve though, by which time, we were a group of ten assembled outside the airport.

Travel fatigue, mixed with the heat, began to take its toll on the conversations and a little bit of loose-change and key jangling in pockets resulted. It was akin to that 'first day at a new school' feeling but with an assorted bunch of apprehensive adults attempting nonchalance.

Luckily, a cheerful, sprightly man soon arrived. He announced himself as Tony, our guide. A powerfully built, squat local man with the organisational skills of the very best a government civil service department might offer, Tony, in a whirlwind of efficiency, had things 'on the go' straightaway.

Within a few minutes our bags had been loaded onto the roof and we all squeezed into a stuffy but character-building minibus.

The *Autoglass* replacement service evidently hadn't yet arrived as we set off with a huge horizontal crack across the windscreen. Neither Tony nor the driver seemed at all perturbed so I relaxed, inhaling the sweaty aroma of long-haul northern European travellers unaccustomed to the equatorial conditions and dreamily surveyed the unfamiliar scenery whilst attempting to breathe mostly through my mouth.

I'd previously been to South Africa where I'd witnessed the stark contrast between First World development and abject poverty that had typified that country, so I was most interested to see if Tanzania was any different.

The route from the airport took us along straight tarmacked roads that seamlessly merged with dusty verges where pedestrians, some carrying impossibly large loads on their heads, freely mixed with motorbikes and lumbering livestock. To me it all appeared slightly haphazard but it functioned perfectly harmoniously. Some of the locals were wearing woolly hats and coats in complete contrast to the hot, sweaty, sticky tourists on our bus who were struggling to stay cool simply wearing shorts and t-shirts.

In the towns, one-storied buildings displayed colourful eye-catching advertisements, some of which were for iconic Western brands, including those which were knowingly obese-making and cancer-causing. How awful that *they* now preyed on these 'innocent' people. Profit and greed over conscience, I presumed. At least the stakeholders are rewarded, so that's ok, isn't it?

And everywhere, satellite dishes were perched on corrugated iron roofs enabling locals to enjoy their football fix as well as, no doubt, to be subjected to the appealing advertisements for even more fattening fast food. It was a fascinating but unsettling mix as the Western advertisements seemed so incongruous compared to the everyday Tanzanian life that was unfolding in front of me. However, there was an ever-constant reassuring air of casual, relaxed serenity and peace that seemed to pervade every town we passed through. No one appeared in a particular hurry. There were no signs of disparities of wealth. I felt very much at ease within my new, unfamiliar, chilled-out environment.

The journey had been mainly on flat, open roads but it finally culminated in a short, sharp doubling-back up a steep bumpy track and after half a mile we arrived at our lodge where we would sleep that night. By now, everyone was exhausted and journey-weary. After reclaiming our bags, there was a short period of hanging around as Tony took care of administrative duties.

Matt and I took the opportunity to try to learn more names from the group to add to Dougie and Steve. We selected a couple of ladies, probably in their late thirties or early forties, who were called Olivia and Karen. I immediately thought of 'olives' and, well, nothing suitable beginning with 'K' revealed itself. I wasn't even convinced that olives were grown in Sub-Saharan Africa.

Also, and I do fully appreciate that beauty is in the eye of the beholder, on first impressions neither of these two ladies, in my most humble, respectful opinion, were oil paintings. In fact, both were more of a collage created from the leftovers at a paint recycling plant. Again, I stress, it was just my opinion. Perhaps I should have simply said, they weren't my type. Either way, I couldn't label them as the 'ugly sisters' in case it slipped out. And then it clicked. It was safer to label them as 'OK' (looking)' - the initials of their names. So that was Olivia and Kate sorted... Karen, rather. They were the 'OK' ladies. Problem solved.

I took some time out away from the conversations in order to fully assess the group. It was reasonably apparent, I guessed, that I was the second oldest in the group of ten and seemingly the ninth fittest in terms of body condition; Dougie way out on his own in tenth and final place in both categories. I felt comfortable with my initial standing in the group.

Soon, we were led into the lodge's grounds and onto a lovely seated veranda area within the complex, complete with wicker furniture, a glass-topped table and a view across a lawn which was surrounded by neatly planted and tendered flower beds bursting with brightly coloured tropical plants. Behind these, were huge towering green trees and shrubs with arching branches and foliage. In the middle of the lawn of thick set, broad-leaved grass was a swimming pool. Initially very appealing, but once through the ant-infested grass and upon closer inspection, the water 'lay' there with an unappealing syrupy chlorine demeanour. It looked rather poorly. During my two days here, I never once saw anyone or anything use this particular facility.

It was briefing time. Tony made it all sound fairly straightforward but, nevertheless, I found it a little daunting. Yes, I'd researched the route endlessly but always from the familiar surroundings and comfort of my own home in England. On paper, on screen it had been only a remote appreciation of the task ahead.

Now, however, we were experiencing a first-hand account of what to expect in an environment full of unfamiliar smells and sounds with no home comforts whatsoever. 'Unfamiliar' can lead to a sense of unease. I felt a little exposed with no bolt hole available to retreat to.

During the team briefing Tony announced that Matt and I had hired the extra thick sleeping mats and that this was a "very good thing to have done." I'd completely forgotten about that but managed a casual smile whilst trying to disguise my immense introspective triumph. I had read about hiring these mats and the fact that they really could make a huge difference when attempting to get some decent sleep or, at the very least, quality rest. They were a couple of inches thick, which would not only provide a degree of comfort on hard rocky surfaces, but would also insulate us against the freezing ground. Hiring them was relatively cheap when compared to the overall cost of the trip and we were not required to carry them, so it had seemed an obvious choice to me.

Also, Matt, using his 'contacts', had sourced a couple of amazing 5-season sleeping bags which really were excellent. He'd 'done a deal' with a local retailer: a very good price in exchange for a photo of Matt atop Kilimanjaro holding one of their branded carrier bags. These sleeping bags would make such a huge difference at higher altitudes. We'd 'tested' them during another trip to South Wales; this time involving tents. Even with the outside night time temperature approaching freezing point, maybe below, we found it possible to cosy up, not together, inside these sleeping bags in only our pants and be perfectly adequately warm.

It's extremely challenging to fall asleep when cold and Tony's words, regarding the mats, had given me an unexpected minor mental boost. I looked forward to the nights of blissful sleeps that undoubtedly lay ahead. It was one less thing to be concerned about.

Midway through the briefing, we were all handed a sketched map of our route. It looked rather similar to Alfred Wainwright's lovingly crafted Lake District drawings.

I'd mulled over so many images of the Lemosho route and read several accounts that I was, by now, immune to the appearance of yet another map no matter how well-intentioned. The map was simply confirming that it would be a very tough challenge, probably the greatest mental and physical feat any average person might face. To be blunt, I just wanted it all to commence. I felt like I was in a doctor's waiting room, waiting to be called for a blood test.

Finally, for those who weren't already travelling as a couple, the group was divided into pairs. It occurred to me that this may have been a slightly anxious moment for some. But, just like *Strictly Come Dancing*, everyone seemed delighted with their partners, contrived or otherwise.

Each pair then headed off to their assigned 'chalet'. These were one-storey cosy brick and wooden structures with a traditional African thatched roof. We were warned that the electricity supply was not always reliable. There were two single beds, each with mosquito nets, something I'd not experienced before, and a bathroom en suite, something I had.

Matt and myself agreed beds, unpacked, freshened-up and excitedly produced our brand spanking new travel adaptors. We then discovered that the wall sockets were the three-pin UK variety, rendering our new purchases totally redundant. One of us - yes, me - had discarded the receipt back at Heathrow Airport so a refund would not be forthcoming. Ooops.

However, to get our money's worth, it would be reasonable justification for another foreign excursion in the future. Rather than 'destination' as our number-one 'search criteria' for our next trip, it would be 'electrical socket requirement'.

So, it was simply a case of plugging our mobile phone chargers directly in and... no electricity! Oh well, we had been warned and, actually, it helped me feel I was somewhere quite remote, which I rather liked, as well as reminding me, in a nostalgic misty-eyed way, of being back home during the 'good old days' of the power cuts during the 1970s. There wasn't time, though, for reminiscing as lunch was being served shortly. So, after taking some more pills for the headache which wasn't shifting, we headed off to find the dining area.

This was now a proper chance to get to know the remaining members of the group. With everyone reasonably refreshed, the atmosphere was far more conducive to chatting.

I'd taken my notebook to lunch and made a few notes about everyone: Andy and Mike were good friends, both in their early thirties, both annoyingly fit with plenty of trekking experience. Simon and Robert, as teamed-up by Tony, were probably in their late thirties and, yes, experienced trekkers. That left Steve who, yep, was also young (I guessed, late twenties) and, yep, a very experienced trekker. 'Fit Steve' I wrote in my notebook. However, Fit Steve had been paired with the not-so-fit Doughnut Dougie. The 'OK' girls were here to mark the occasion of and to celebrate Karen's (or was it Kate's) fortieth birthday which was in a few days' time.

Consequently, I'd now discovered that I was easily the least experienced trekker. Did it bother me? Well, if I'm honest, it did a little bit. But then I reminded myself that I'd spent five months of gruelling preparation (admittedly by my own very modest standards) shaking off thirty odd years of inactivity and I'd arrived ready for action sporting a ripped Adonis-like body... when compared to Dougie.

So, with personal reassurances on a relative high, it wasn't long before I was tucking into a most wonderful, home-cooked burger with fresh salad, accompanied by a warm vinaigrette, which had neatly separated in the sun. I was blatantly ignoring the advice to avoid salads at all costs. "If it's not cooked, peeled or boiled then don't eat it" was yet another item to remember from my exhaustive research list of dos and definitely don'ts. However, I'm a stickler for my 'five a day' and couldn't pass up on this opportunity. Consequently, I permitted myself this risky tick in the 'definitely don't' column.

After lunch there was the option of a local walk. Both Matt and myself decided to opt out, preferring an 'afternoon in' of rest following the weariness of long-distance travelling. I'm pretty sure we both fell asleep within only a few minutes of lying down on our beds.

Waking up at 17:15, I was very disheartened to discover my headache was continuing to bother me and consequently swallowed yet more tablets. Fortunately, due to reading all about altitude sickness, I'd packed a ridiculous amount of paracetamol. Perhaps more importantly, electricity had rediscovered our chalet and so, frantically, we placed our phones on charge in case it was a mere fleeting luxury.

By 18:45 we had all reconvened in the bar ahead of the evening meal. The afternoon walk had been enjoyed by six members of the group. I was ever so slightly concerned that they may have gained a competitive advantage over me. I gently reprimanded myself to remember that this wasn't a race or a competition and that, in actual fact, this would be a team effort with everyone fully supporting each other.

We all enjoyed a beer or two with a wholesome meal; nothing excessive. Now, with everyone in a much more relaxed frame of mind, personalities began to emerge like a mountain peak appearing through the swirling mist (how appropriate... or was it simply a metaphor to suggest the presence of an underlying concern).

The only other residents that evening was a boisterous group of Chinese hikers who had just returned from their own attempt at Kilimanjaro. I tried to ask of one of them a question but it soon became apparent that none spoke English and I certainly had no words of Mandarin whatsoever.

They were all in very high spirits (perhaps they'd all summitted, I thought) and were being royally entertained by a live African band who were playing songs with ridiculous numbers of verses that went on and on and on...

Our group, on the other hand, were relatively sedate, attempting to quietly get to know each other better.

By the time we left the dining area at 22:00, the lubricated Chinese hikers had somehow managed to commandeer the microphone and were participating in their own wild, raucous karaoke session. Their songs also went on and on and on... It looked as though they might continue for quite some time. The African band had clearly buggered off.

I should have expected this, but back at our chalet, the electricity was off again so we were forced to get ready for bed by torchlight. Romantic? It wasn't. Instead, it was actually quite challenging, what with clothes and stuff sacks strewn everywhere. Yep, hands up, mostly mine. OK, all.

Amidst the rummaging kerfuffle, an enormous moth flew in through an open window. Bugger, we should have shut that on the way out for the evening meal. Nevertheless, we were both reasonably comfortable with the presence of this hand-sized visitor especially as neither of us had read about a threat of poisonous or killer ones. So long as it remained on the outside of the mosquito net there would be no concerns. We'd all get along fine in our own designated comfort zones. Besides, this rather beautifully decorated bobowler would keep my mind off the deadly venomous snake that was undoubtedly coiled under my mattress.

Once in bed, safely snuggled under a duvet and shielded by a net, I relaxed and waited to nod off. However, rather annoyingly a mosquito had also broken into our room and its high-pitched whining was immediately irritating. In the pitch dark, I could sense it knew exactly where I was but my net was holding firm. I prayed there wasn't a hole in it.

I am, unfortunately, a target for all manner of flying bitey things. I believe it might have something to do with any or all of the following: my blood group; giving off more carbon dioxide than most people; running a hot body temperature; or the bacteria on my skin. According to a report I read, Professor Jonathan Day of the University of Florida categorises people like me as "high attractor types." I think that translates as a 'Mozzie Magnet'.

After a few minutes, the mozzie went quiet. That, actually, made matters worse. I now wondered what it was up to. Perhaps it was chewing its way through the net? Gone for back-up? Not that it would matter too much as I was sporting a fair amount of *DEET*, sufficient to deep-fry myself in, and was taking a course of *Malarone* tablets. I almost felt inclined to let the bugger in, feast on me, and then fly off. At least that way we could both get on with our lives.

Next on the conveyor belt of nocturnal annoyances was frenzied activity in our roof. I've never had a thatch to contend with but knew that it would make a perfect habitat for a variety of African creatures. 'Mad Mandy' had always lived with a tufty thatch and that was constantly inhabited with crabs.

Staring up into the pitch dark from my bed, I convinced myself that it definitely wasn't a snake or large spider making all that noise. It must have been a small mammal or reptile. I was sure it was outside; so that was ok, wasn't it? I'll never, ever moan about a house spider back in England again.

After a couple of hours of drifting in and out of sleep, I finally succumbed to the call of my bladder. So, first, it was headtorch on. Next, I fought the folds of the mosquito net to eventually break through and then navigated my way past our belongings on the floor, tip-toed over the snakes, and into the bathroom where there was an instant scurry of padded feet. Was there no end to this night time torturous teasing?

And there it was, on the wall high above the sink - a gecko. I had managed not to shout out or scream but my heart was racing. I was *fairly* certain that I wasn't in any danger, it was purely the surprise factor that had alarmed me. However, in case this uninvited inhabitant did have the ability to jump across the room and 'go for the throat', I very slowly and deliberately backed my way into the toilet cubicle not once taking my eyes off the potential assassin.

I was now trying to pee under severe pressure. I felt sure that 'it' would dart across the ceiling and position itself above my head ready to pounce or maybe just unnervingly stare at me with its big bulging, unblinking eyes. And, having one hand fully occupied, I would surely be a sitting duck for the reptilian assailant.

However, all remained quiet and still and I was able to relieve myself taking this opportunity to diligently inspect the colour of my wee. Under the spotlight of my headtorch, I could tell it was definitely a tad on the dark side so I knew I'd have to increase my intake of water.

Back in the bedroom and after a fisherman's-like account of what had just happened, by which time the gecko was now 3-foot long, armed with vicious teeth and claws, and had got me by the throat, Matt casually told me to "grow a pair". It's a classic, laconic, male mates' way

57

of simultaneously displaying both concern and sympathy so I was happily calmed. Very soon, with a gentle prod from the sleepy stick, I felt myself drifting off to… and then the bloody mosquito started whining again.

Chapter 5 – Day 1. The adventure begins

Following a night of rest but very little actual sleep, it was everyone up at 06:00 and a moment of relief and joy as I realised my headache had finally cleared.

I wasn't expecting any electricity... and there wasn't, so I couldn't really justify feeling any disappointment at not being able to illuminate the room by means of flicking a light switch.

It made packing in the dim light quite challenging though. The packing, unpacking, filling of stuff sacks, attempting a logical approach, and perpetually trying to remember where everything was located was already becoming quite tiresome. Being an organised traveller was evidently not a strength of mine

Over breakfast, we learned that those in the chalets closer to the reception area had not experienced any break in their electricity supply at all. Hmm, something to bear in mind if I ever returned.

Before setting off 'properly', we each had the opportunity to leave items at the lodge before packing our rucksacks with our daily requirements plus one kit bag of up to 15kg in weight. The kit bags would be transported by our amazing porters all the way up to the final camp and back down again, hence the strict weight allowance.

With the exception of Matt, everyone came in at or under the maximum allowance. Ok, hands up, I admit that Matt's bag now contained one mangled moth, one muffled mozzie and a garrotted gecko but come on! Anyway, at 16kg, Matt's bag was permitted onboard with a broad smile and ironic anger.

And so, two days after leaving England, we were finally heading off to tackle our daunting challenge. I was like a child on Christmas Eve, simply bursting with excitement. I could not wait to begin hiking up the mountain.

Setting off at 08:45, we were transported in two groups and after approximately an hour our Land Rovers turned off the main road and onto a reasonably flat dirt track. Soon, beginning to rise gently upwards, we passed through a handful of small towns. Once again, these were a familiar mix of timbered structures with pitched corrugated iron roofs upon which were seated satellite dishes all uniformly angled like meerkats on alert. Motorbikes mixed with market stall vendors and pedestrians. The apparent chaos, to my unaccustomed eyes, unfolded in a perfect serenely choreographed order. What else should I have expected by now? I was falling for Tanzania.

Presently, we arrived at the first gate to the park. I wasn't sure what I was expecting but I certainly didn't anticipate a seemingly token length of rusty chain, precariously held eighteen inches off the ground and manned by one official who was sat dreamily in a wooden 'office'. How unremarkable. To be fair, though, there was a bright red hazard triangle attached to the top of a short stump proudly on display in the middle of a tiny grassy 'traffic island'. I concede *that* portrayed a semblance of officialdom.

After a brief discussion, presumably helping to justify the officer's occupation, the chain was casually lowered by hand and we drove through.

Back home I had read that, apparently, this is where the park fees were paid to the Forest Authority but I still remain surprised by how unassuming it all was. The chain was then quickly raised as if he was anticipating a deluge of visitors, and the chap ambled back to the comfort of his hut. Once again, I felt reminded of the way things work around here. I was genuinely warming to this more informal way of life.

The track was now a rich reddish-brown colour and sufficiently bumpy to suggest we were heading somewhere wild. Having said that, it was not altogether dissimilar to negotiating the pot-holed A-roads at home.

Not long afterwards I caught my first striking glimpse of a classic black and white Colobus monkey going about its business high up in a nearby tree. Again, not totally dissimilar but eminently more pleasing and alive than the striking site of a black and white badger, turned roadkill, at home.

Almost simultaneously the unmistakable olfactory evidence of someone 'faring well' presented itself within the confines of my nasal passages. From the safety of my very limited personal space within the Land Rover and without any overt movements of my head but, instead, with spy-like glances, I inspected the fellow passengers for signs of guilt. I knew it wasn't Matt; we always tell each other when we've let one go or at the very least raise a silent Roger Moore-warning eyebrow accompanied with slightly narrowing eyes.

The chief suspect, shifting his weight from buttock to buttock and looking far into the distance in an attempt to, literally, throw us off the scent, was Dougie! If we'd have been playing *Cluedo*, I'd most certainly have declared my accusation there and then: 'it was Dougie, in the Land Rover, with his arse!'

At 10:45 we reached the significant presence of the Londorossi Gate which, did indeed, possess a metal gate neatly framed by two vertical wooden poles and a cross beam at the top. No sorry-looking rusty chain here at the official registration point for the Lemosho Route. We had officially entered Kilimanjaro National Park. It was a welcome opportunity to disembark and to stretch dozing leg muscles. Our guide set off on his administrative duties leaving us to wander around and breathe in the fresh mountain air.

Small pots of cacti and brightly coloured flowers were decoratively positioned where grass verges surrendered to dusty tracks. This outpost appeared to have been constructed entirely from wood. It wouldn't have been out of keeping if Clint Eastwood and Lee Van Cleef had charged in on horseback, entered the saloon, ordered a whisky - "and make it a large one" - shot a bandit and had it away with the buxom barmaid. Then, the previously startled pianist would have commenced playing again.

Whilst hikers enjoyed the chance to mill around, bags were being weighed and porters were bartering for business in a frenzy of activity. I was pleased that our support crew had already been appointed and was somewhere nearby so we didn't have to engage in the melee.

One of the prominent landmarks here is a huge sign titled 'Points to Remember' giving one final warning to all those who planned to venture further.

The hypochondriac hiker who lives inside my rucksack tried to convince me that I had every reason to turn around: go back to the safety of your comfort zone! What have you let yourself in for? This isn't for you!

However, the intrepid explorer bulging in my handy zip-off trousers fought back after reading point number three: "Children under 10 years of age are not allowed above 3,000 metres." I had cleared ten years of age many years ago and so passed that 'test' with flying colours. Number six was *most* intriguing: "Do not push yourself to go if your body is exhausted or if you have extreme". Extreme what was the obvious question but no one felt inclined to ask. Best left at that.

There were other slightly worrying phrases, such as "physically fit", "breathing problems", "heart or lung problems", "consulting your doctor", "mountain sickness", "high altitude diseases", "descend immediately and seek medical treatment". However, I'd prepared assiduously for five whole months and nothing was going to stop me. So, I fronted-up by turning around, wearing a faked air of extreme nonchalance and confidence, walking away and looking for inadequately prepared fat people for whom this sign might have some obvious relevancy. Other than Dougie, there weren't any. Everyone else appeared remarkably svelte and very well kitted-out.

We were all summoned to complete the necessary but, nonetheless, tedious and, at times tricky, admin task of answering so many questions during a form-filling process. Like many people, I quite happily fill out forms without properly reading any of the details. Some questions are occasionally rather taxing and it's often easier simply to make-up responses. In doing so, I'm led to believe that I have already bequeathed my house, my children and six kidneys.

Today was no exception and, with everything going on around me being so ridiculously unfamiliar, I was completely overwhelmed by the whole experience. In my bewilderment, I seem to recall referring to my passport at one stage as a prompt for the answer to the 'nationality' question. Once over, I'd probably signed away yet another kidney to a worthy cause.

I presumed all our personal information, such as ages and nationalities, was being used for, not only statistical purposes, but also as a check that the numbers of people entering the Park equally matched those departing; hopefully.

Tedious part over, we climbed back onboard the Land Rovers and headed off again. The 'Points to Remember' sign hadn't warned us of the immediate peril of the condition of the track and we were soon thrown, tossed and pitched around inside the vehicle like lottery balls; and with the usual bad luck - or was it... at one stage I felt sure I had one of Karen's nipples in my mouth. Admittedly, not unpleasant, but this wasn't really a conducive environment in which to fully appreciate such pleasures. Better than Dougie's arse though, I thought to myself.

The track appeared impossibly rutted, far, far worse than your Gran's hairy top lip. On several occasions I honestly felt sure we would tip over. Who knows what would have ended up in my mouth then? As long as it didn't belong to Dougie I really didn't care too much.

And then we stopped abruptly.

Our guide and driver stepped out of the vehicle. A puncture! So, everyone was required to vacate the vehicle while the wheel was changed. It afforded us an unscheduled opportunity to: stretch legs, fart, pee and overcome the feeling of lottery ball-induced seasickness. All of us took full advantage of this pitstop. In fact, I ticked-off all four as did Dougie, I reckon, judging by his contented grin.

There had been no more stops until we arrived at our destination deep in the equatorial forest. The other half of our group had already been there twenty minutes and, naturally, wondered why it had taken us so long. The explanation caused them much amusement even without divulging the farting and misplaced nipple incidents. It was another early sign of how altitude makes things far funnier than at sea level. I would suggest that emerging comedians (even rubbish ones) would gain early confidence by performing at altitude. Trust me, your audience will laugh at anything… unless they're suffering from mountain sickness.

It was now the first meeting of the whole team: our athletic, tightly-coiled, simply raring-to-go group of eight, the guides, the porters, the chef, and myself and Dougie.

Due to a tropical cocktail of trepidation, anticipation, adrenalin and a slight feeling of inadequacy I permitted myself an unperceptively quiet comfort fart - a modest little one, similar in effect to the gin and tonic 'settler' Matt and I had enjoyed back at Heathrow but without the 'ice and a slice'. It certainly did the trick and I considered my acclimatisation process had increased a notch. I was perhaps 'ahead of the game' now; definitely ahead of Dougie. But it was NOT a competition, I reminded myself.

I do appreciate that the subject of farting is not to everyone's liking. But even at this early stage, it was becoming increasingly apparent that it was in fact a normal and wholly expected bodily function at altitude. It really did become an integral part of this trip. That was the reality of the situation. And, for all of us, it was also the source of much amusement; the scale beginning at 'amusing' and, at times, peaking at 'hilarity'.

Asim announced himself as our head guide, introduced his assistant guides and presented the support crew. Most were wearing everyday clothing such as t-shirts, sweaters, woolly hats and some had footwear that I considered inadequate for the environment that lay ahead: boots with holes in the toes, plimsols and even sandals.

It reinforced my plan, also suggested in Henry's guidebook, to leave behind as much gear as possible for them after I'd finished with it.

They sported, of course, a range of football shirts, predominantly Manchester United, Liverpool, Chelsea and Barcelona, not that any of them would have ever had the chance to attend a live game. Even in this relatively remote area of Africa, the power and effect of satellite TV on a truly global audience was evident.

Our support team were all from the African Walking Company (AWC), a local operator whose primary objectives, other than helping climbers to summit Kilimanjaro, is to provide the highest levels of working conditions for their staff and care of the environment.

As we would discover, the guides all speak English, have a career path within the company and have invaluable experience of the mountain. Our guides had all begun their careers as porters and then progressed to assistant guide or head guide. They typically expect to summit Kili (they have earned the right to refer to it as 'Kili') twenty times each year! I was simply aiming for once in a lifetime.

The equipment they carry for the climbers is of a very high standard with, amongst other things, sturdy 3-man tents for each pair of guests, aluminium dining chairs, full medical kits, an emergency oxygen system and a luxury blue team toilet tent.

The food provided each day is nothing short of miraculous and is carefully prepared in order to contain an essential high liquid and carbohydrate content.

Any rubbish generated by the group is collected on a daily basis, carried by the porters and eventually disposed of once back off the mountain again.

On top of all of this, and without exception, each guide and porter was so incredibly friendly, happy and supportive, and only too willing to motivate and help us through their advice, songs and huge smiles. It was impossible not to fall in love with each and every one of them... and I did, cos I'm like that.

On the subject of the incredible food, I did find a summary which accurately reflected my experience, on www.ganeandmarshall.com, of what might be expected on a typical day using the AWC.

Daily Meals:
Bed Tea - tea or coffee served in your tent.

Breakfast consists of seasonal fresh fruit (mango/banana/watermelon), porridge, cooked eggs, sausage, bacon and toast.

Energy snacks are provided for the daily walk such as biscuits, bananas, and chocolate bars.

Lunch is either a packed lunch on longer days or, more usually, a hot lunch served in camp by a small team who have raced ahead of the clients. A hot lunch typically consists of soup, bread or pancakes, cheese, tuna, jam, peanut butter, pasta salad and cake.

Afternoon tea is served in late afternoon. It is an opportunity to drink lots of hot drinks and snack on peanuts or popcorn.

Dinner is the main meal of the day and always consists of three courses; soup and bread, followed by a main dish, which could be rice, potatoes or pasta with fish, meat or vegetables, and is followed by a dessert often of fruit.

One useful point I will add relates to the recommended daily intake of water. Most research states that 4-5 litres of water should be consumed in order to help ward off the potentially nasty effects of altitude. Rather cleverly, one litre (at the very least) of that daily target is usually attained simply at meal times through the likes of soup, vegetables, fruit and, of course, the various drinks on offer.

This certainly reduced the, at times, onerous pressure of constantly trying to drink the target amount from one's own water supply, especially as the taste of boiled and sterilised water becomes quite tedious after a few days. Not only did the water, for me, develop an unappealing sanitised flavour with slight chemical undertones from, at least one of, the halogen elements (gosh, I should be a wine critic) but I'm convinced it began to upset my stomach. By that stage, even the swimming pool water back at the lodge would have been an alternative worthy of consideration.

The AWC is a partner of the Kilimanjaro Porters Assistance Project (KPAP). According to their website (https://kiliporters.org/), they were established in 2003 and are a legally registered Tanzanian not-for-profit organisation. Their mission is to improve the working conditions of the porters on Kilimanjaro.

Additionally, I would like to quote:
"Promoting Socially Responsible Kilimanjaro Climbs.
Those who have climbed Mount Kilimanjaro know that porters are the backbone of the trek. Many climbers may not realize that porters can be ill-equipped, poorly paid and have improper working conditions. KPAP's focus is improving the working conditions of the porters by:

- *Lending mountain clothing to porters free of charge*
- *Advocating for fair wages and ethical treatment by all companies climbing Kilimanjaro*
- *Encouraging climbers to select a climbing company with responsible treatment practices towards their crew*
- *Providing educational opportunities to the mountain crew"*

If you are considering tackling Kilimanjaro, I feel very strongly that you should use companies who are partnered with the AWC and KPAP; most well-established tour operators seem to be.

In all, there appeared to be approximately 30 members of our support team - a mixture of assistant guides, porters and one remarkable chef. Each one was a hero in my eyes.

Fortunately, throughout the whole trip, there was plenty of time to talk to Asim and his assistant guides, and some porters too. I was so pleased and felt immensely rewarded that I'd grasped this opportunity.

As a consequence of the birth lottery, the chances of our life-paths ever crossing were minute. But, here we all were, a disparate group from different cultures, backgrounds, upbringings, religions and beliefs immediately, and with no hesitation at all, forging deep bonds of genuine friendship.

And, here was I, an awkward Englishman far removed from my comfort zone, talking to local Tanzanians as if we had been life-long friends. It was rather similar to my experiences of talking to 'strangers' in Ireland; as the wonderful Irish poet, WB Yeats, once wrote: "There are no strangers, only friends you have not met yet."

Sadly, our human race as an entity is still unable to fully live or even adequately cope with differences, such as colour, religion, race and sexuality but throughout my travels I've always been heartened by how remarkably similar the overwhelming majority of us are at a basic fundamental human level. We all cry, grieve, smile and laugh. Strip away the leaders, labels, borders and resultant ill-informed prejudices and suspicions and we're all pretty much the same. I've exchanged knowing looks and smiles with people whom I've not been able to verbally communicate with. There's a common, deep-rooted bond between us all.

I resolutely believe that travelling, learning about unfamiliar cultures, not being judgemental, being respectful of different customs, experiencing first-hand new societies and for, at least a brief while, integrating into it, and generally being friendly and polite are things we can all do to establish harmony for everyone. In no small measure, a big smile and a knowledge of football has always helped me too.

I do get labelled a hippy by some friends but I simply regard myself as a child of our one Mother Earth... yeah, ok, I am a bit of an old hippy. I live in hope that the world will be as one. *Imagine* that.

We later discovered that some of our guides and porters had been on that 2009 *Comic Relief* trek, led by Gary Barlow; whom, they reported, had been a perfect gent! They were so pleased to share their stories of the trek and, by association, their claims to modest fame. We even got to hear the odd snippets of gossip but, and slightly adapting the well-known saying - 'what goes on tour, stays on tour' – 'what goes on the mountain, stays on the mountain', so I won't say a thing. The whole group of celebrities and their crew had been a great bunch to be with. It sounded like a most memorable trip.

By 12:45, we had picked up our rucksacks and were following Asim along a dusty path, leaving the support crew to burden themselves with our kit bags. Although the initial part of the hike was reasonably flat, I found myself breathing quite heavily. This was at *only* five-and-a-half 'Worcestershire Beacons' (WBs) - my new unit of measurement to help me 'visualise' heights on this crazy trip. It was my first proper encounter with the effects of altitude but it didn't take too long before the going and my breathing became much easier again. I realised I was 'acclimatising'!

Start of trek – Mti Mkubwa

Soon, Mekeke, one of the assistant guides, alerted our attention to a chameleon. Unless we have the absolute masters of disguise in the British countryside, this was the first chameleon I'd ever seen in the wild. However, he was possibly having an off day. Our reclining reptile was sporting a most fetching pattern of brown, olive, fawn and luminous highlighter pen yellow. He was casually basking on an all-green offshoot of what might have been Jack's beanstalk. He'd completely and utterly failed to blend in with the vegetation he was perched upon. Was he colour blind? Was he nailed there like a parrot? A momentary thrilling sight all the same and all ten of our group must have each taken a dozen photographs of this brazen beauty.

There had, already, been so many new thrilling sights and sounds. I was so excited to be in Tanzania but, at this current rate of photographic profligacy, it was going to take us the best part of a whole year to complete our trip.

Mekeke then pointed out Mount Meru behind us... another dozen photos each! It must have been a few miles away but, nevertheless, looked impressively striking wearing its own scarf of cloud. I was aware of this 'sister peak' and knew it was in the region of 4,500 metres in height and that some hardy trekkers use it as a warm up to the main event, Kilimanjaro, something that I could never have entertained.

I asked the guide how far away it was. He replied, "about 70 kilometres". Being old school, to fully appreciate that distance, I had to perform some mental arithmetic and converted the figure into just over 40 miles! Surely not? To appear so imposing at that distance away established yet another result: mild shock. It was probably best to merely shrug that one off. I chose to 'un-see' it.

We ambled on at a slow walk. It was clear, right from the very off, that the pace was going to be slow today. It matched the advice in all the books to take it slowly. It suited me perfectly. I could sense, though, that the younger members of the group, that is everyone with the exception of myself and Dougie, were simply champing at the bit like greyhounds waiting for the hare - yes, I know! Racehorses would have been a more appropriate simile. The Editor has clearly missed it; probably having her hair or nails done.

The atmosphere was hot and dry; probably in the high twenty degrees. There was no breeze at all and heavy clouds, effectively acting as a lid on a pan, ensured the temperature would remain constant for quite some time. Thankfully, the slow pace meant that none of us was dripping in sweat but armpits and brows were most certainly on the wetter side of moist.

So, it came as a most welcome treat when we stopped for a break under the shade of the forest canopy. We drank as much water as we could, mindful of the 'required' daily dosage as prescribed by all the guide books, chewed snacks and gently chatted.

I'd been happily farting freely during the walk so far, so too had Matt. Mates are good at that. No embarrassment whatsoever. In fact, it even gets competitive at times. Whilst sat snacking, I did perceive Andy and Mike also indulging in a spot of windy activity. Everyone else seemed far too reserved to release their 'faring well' inhibitions. I was convinced that would change as the trip advanced.

It wasn't too long before the first members of the support team came cheerfully marching past us, effortlessly carrying all the gear which included tents, chairs, mats, huge water flagons, our kit bags and all sorts of other paraphernalia. Most were carrying these items on their heads, some had back packs, and others even had both!

It was truly humbling, and ever so slightly embarrassing, to see these slight figures carrying loads that I certainly could not have struggled with for more than a hundred feet or so. Not only that, they were chatting, laughing, smiling and occasionally singing!

We never failed to marvel at these extraordinary people. Our deep respect and gratitude towards them increased day by day. They performed hugely impressive feats, every single day, every single one of them. I can assure you, dear reader, that by the end of the week we all felt that no matter what size of tip we collected as a group for them, it would never be sufficient reward for their gargantuan efforts in helping us achieve our ultimate goal.

As the trek continued, we entered a predominantly forested area which presented, what I presumed was, high humidity. This, for me, was a completely new experience: heat with significant invisible volumes of added moisture thrown into the mix, all held in suspension by the ubiquitous lush green vegetation. The result, was to induce all-over body sweating and a shirt that barely had a dry patch on it after only a few minutes. At least I'd commenced today with my 'zippable' trousers zipped-off at the knees; the exposed sweat on my lower legs performing a reasonable cooling effect.

Ever since visiting The Eden Project (described as "a dramatic global garden housed in tropical biomes" by www.visitcornwall.com), in Cornwall, in the UK, I'd longed to experience proper equatorial conditions for 'real'. In the Cornish version I'd worn shorts and a t-shirt so to me these seemed wholly appropriate for the 'real thing': the Tanzanian tropical climate.

The forest path was narrow, resulting in a weaving, undulating single-file procession of hikers, guides and porters. Single-file meant that any points of interest were passed down the line, from Asim at the front, from person to person in a snake-like digestive act, with much pointing and transference of information in a Chinese whispers fashion; not always producing an accurate result. On one occasion, a bird in a tree, known as a 'Hartlaub's turaco' had morphed into a 'hot tub chorizo'?

By the time a hypnotic ants' highway, with a cast of millions, was brought to my intention, I was naively stood within their main arterial route and had become their service station. At that moment, I *so* wished that I'd been wearing long trousers *and* had tucked them securely into my socks.

I didn't scream or panic as I viewed 'them', in horror, trampling *all* over my boots, with some venturing further and exploring my bare legs. Instead, Matt helped me very gently brush them off with impressive finesse and we quickly moved on as though nothing had happened.

On subsequent visits to equatorial jungle environments, I have always worn long trousers. And, following a shocking, stomach-churning leech incident, long sleeves too!

I simply could not eradicate the sensation of the crawling ants. Medically known as formication, it was causing me to perpetually shake my arms and legs as we negotiated the path. Surely, 'they' were inside my pants too and venturing unnervingly into deeply personal territory.

Even though I was blissfully unaware, for the very first time in my life, I was 'shaking my booty'.

Respite eventually came in the form of the mesmerising distraction of a balletic display from incandescent butterflies effortlessly fluttering among the vegetation. They are beautiful creatures, my favourites, seemingly so delicate with their dainty gossamer wings yet they are able to thrive in sometimes unforgiving and potentially dangerous environments. This juxtaposition made me admire them even more. One in particular caught a shard of sunlight and sparkled like a diamond among emeralds in Ali Baba's cave. I was hopelessly captivated. I could have watched her alluring spectacle for much longer but, sadly, we had to press on deeper into the forest.

As we progressed, the group spread out into three separate groups as a natural order of the fittest was beginning to be established: There were 'the fit ones', which included Matt, as the pioneering lead-team. With 'Pole, Pole' permanently at the forefront of my mind, I was more than happy to be in my own 'group of one', totally contented with going at my own comfortable pace.

Lastly, a puffing, panting ruby-faced Dougie had formed his own 'solo breakaway team' at the rear but judging by his repeated porcine noises I wasn't totally convinced that he was altogether contented. His lack of fitness, though, had gained him a personal guide in the form of Mekeke; it was a rather fortunate, for him, but totally unplanned consequence of not being fully prepared for the trip.

During adventures such as this one, it is inevitable that a group will consist of mixed abilities and speeds. Therefore, it's imperative not to worry about 'being left behind' or being slow. The Kilimanjaro trek is not a race. Its objective is to get from point-to-point each day in the best way one can, and at all times a guide will either be hiking with and chatting to everyone as part of the team, setting the pace which is appropriate for the individual or group or discretely keeping an eye on things from a reasonable distance as the group members set their own speeds.

I felt very much in safe hands at all times. These guys were all highly trained and vastly experienced. Their presence was non-invasive yet hugely reassuring. A perfect mix.

After three-and-a-quarter hours of hiking upwards across five miles, occasionally quite steeply, I was the ninth member of the team to reach camp. I presumed the pioneering lead-team had been there for quite some time but, to my surprise, I was only a few minutes behind them.

I permitted myself a modest pat on the back. I felt fine, not out of breath and certainly not tired; probably overdosing on adrenalin and the novelty factor. This was the Big Tree Camp, also known as Mti Mkubwa or simply the Forest Camp. At 2,785 metres (9,137 feet, or six-and-a-half WBs) it was the highest I'd ever been on foot.

I did glance around the camp for a particularly tall or big tree but was slightly disappointed to observe that actually they were all fairly tall and big! It was only when I returned home and did some post-trip research that I learned: firstly, this camp was Big Tree Camp as opposed to *The* Big Tree Camp. So, I should have expected several big trees, which is exactly what was on show. Secondly, those 'big trees' are *Podocarpus usambarensis*, a type of conifer tree which grows in highland rain forests from an altitude of between 950 and 2,700 metres. Any pedants reading this may recall that Big Tree Camp is in fact at an altitude of 2,785 metres – just let it go!

These trees grow up to 60 metres in height and are "many-branched" with a compact crown. That would explain the predominance of cool shadowy shade at the camp which was very welcome to our group of still-acclimatising, not used to this sort of heat, sweaty Brits.

Interestingly, in the UK, it is said that the highest recorded tree - a Douglas fir, growing somewhere near Inverness - stands at 66.4 metres! No Scottish - our tree's taller than your tree - gloating could be justified though, as we were already standing at more than twice the height of Ben Nevis.

Asim led us to the green, circular, pitched-roofed ranger's hut where we had to sign-in, including details such as age, nationality and occupation. It was a less formal version of the procedure that had been required of us when we had entered the Park, at Londorossi Gate, earlier that day.

Just as we'd completed our administrative formalities Dougie arrived impersonating a grunty sweaty African warthog, accompanied by the ever-patient, always smiling, not a drop of sweat on him, Mekeke.

The tenth member of our team was welcomed with generous smiles all round as he mopped his dripping wet facial features. In exactly the same way as a 'Miss Wet t-shirt' competition, apparently (cough, cough), leaves nothing to the imagination, so too were Dougie's generous moobs brazenly on show through his skin-tight tee. They glided effortlessly from side to side with blancmange-like motion under his drenched shirt. 'Dougie Does Dallas' sprang to my mind. Altitude reaping havoc once again!

Amazingly, our five lime-green and purple tents with fetching tangy orange interiors had already been erected in a neat row. Matt chose our cosy dwelling for the night. It was the 'residence' closest to our mess tent. Once again, Matt had displayed his undoubted 'outdoor' skills, leaving us with only a 20-foot stroll to the 'restaurant'. Our nearest 'neighbours', Andy and Mike, were faced with all of twenty-five feet.

Inside our cosy tent, I proceeded to unpack and roll out my even cosier sleeping bag. Then I spewed the remaining contents of my rucksack and kit bag into the 'neutral zone' in the centre of our tent. Matt gave me a look that, if politely translated into words, would have said, "That's possibly not the best way to go about things." But, hey, that was me rapidly sorted. And, as it turned out, just in time for tea and salted popcorn which was now being served in the jolly nearby mess tent.

This unexpected treat wasn't mandatory but all of us took full advantage of the generous offering. Thinking ahead to when appetites would inevitably fail us at higher altitudes, I presumed future popcorn might be served then as an irresistible source of energy. For now, though, it was simply a treat.

The consumption of calories on this trip is extremely important. For most people, this will be the most physically demanding venture of their lives. Due to my research, I was fully aware that one rather cruel side-effect of altitude is that it can diminish one's appetite just when you need it the most. So, I considered it wise to eat anything and everything that was on offer at the beginning of the trip. I was effectively building up a 'reserve' should my appetite fail me later on.

As we shared the enormous popcorn portions and passed around the flasks of tea, the general chat turned to everyone's experiences of the trip so far as well as past adventures. It soon became apparent that Matt and myself were complete novices compared to the rest of the seasoned worldwide travellers in the group especially as our past hiking and camping experiences had been confined to the UK.

However, what they didn't realise was that at home, Matt was a Master of Rural Ramblings. He'd been wild camping on many occasions. He could easily start a fire, boil some water and prepare the veg whilst skinning a rabbit with his feet and all this from within a canoe negotiating white water rapids by means of one strategically placed oar.

As for me, well, I could now erect a tent without having to refer to the instructions and walk a lot without whinging, oh, and always be relied upon to have a flask of RSJ-strength builder's tea and a morale-boosting chunky chocolate bar or two. We were a good, if slightly, one-sided team.

Clearly, the others in our group weren't in the slightest bit overawed by our situation. I, on the other hand, was absolutely, truly, utterly gobsmacked, almost to that point of pinching myself. I was in Tanzania and that morning had not only trekked through an equatorial forest but had witnessed creatures in their own habitats that I'd only previously seen in a zoo or a book.

I was on an expedition - me, on an expedition, a proper one - with real guides and real porters. Unreal! And now, I was in a mess tent eating popcorn - a snack I had only ever previously associated with trips to the cinema - with experienced 'explorers' flanking me, having completed my first few steps up Kilimanjaro.

With a nonchalant poker face portraying a man of vast worldly experience, I think I disguised my incredulity rather well. However, behind my Royal Flush, I was simply bursting to run around sharing my hand with everyone in camp in a childlike frenzy of excitement and ruining my chances of winning a big pot of money.

The camp appeared to have the ranger's hut centrally located with groups of tents dotted all around in amongst the big trees. There were more tents than I'd expected, at least thirty or more, spread over a 50-yard radius, suggesting we'd joined maybe half a dozen similar sized groups of hikers to our own. The camp may have been bigger but it was impossible to fully gauge due to all those big trees. Surely, Man should have cut them all down, made an attractive clearing and rendered all the wildlife homeless, no?

To the consternation of my bowel region, I'd only so far spotted one infamous 'long-drop' toilet. It was my first ever sighting so I was fascinated by its appearance: a wooden rectangular structure, approximately 8-feet tall and 6-feet wide and deep; not dissimilar to a modest garden shed. This 'model' featured a slanted wooden roof, raised by means of four short pieces of timber on each corner which, I presumed, provided a certain degree of al fresco ventilation. This gap, worryingly, was also wide enough to permit entry to a wide range of jungle fauna. However, that concern was rendered redundant when I realised there was no hinged door anyway. Entry was by means of a 3-foot wide opening, allowing free access to anything, into a disturbingly dark interior prompting images, in my mind, of the Minotaur's labyrinth.

I wondered, with itching curiosity (it could have been the ants) what the inside was like. I'll wager someone has written a thesis on these notorious thrones. However, this wooden monument wasn't a tourist attraction and I was no Theseus, so I resisted the temptation to potter around inside and take photos to show the folks back home. Besides, our own personal blue team toilet tent had been erected nearby so, come the 'movement' moment, *that* would certainly be my preferred port of call.

At 18:00 we were summoned to the evening meal. The light was already beginning to fade but it was conducive to a homely atmosphere, further enhanced when Asim fixed a warm, glowing solar lamp to the ceiling.

I'd read a great number of complimentary reviews concerning the food provided on this particular trip so was eager and excited to sample the fayre.

Courgette soup followed by fried chicken, boiled potatoes and spinach was quite extraordinarily delicious especially considering where we were - part way up a dormant volcano - and the kind of 'kitchen', presumably a tent, it had all been prepared and cooked in.

I completed the meal with both a sense of astonishment and a completely satisfied stomach. The reviews had been spot-on. This Big Tree Restaurant fully warranted the Michelin mountain culinary star that I appreciatively awarded it.

After the telltale empty plates had been cleared away and hot drinks served, Asim addressed the group to firstly find out how everyone was feeling and, secondly, to brief us on the following day's itinerary. He made it quite clear we were to alert him *immediately* to any headaches, cuts - for fear of infection - or any other niggles.

Asim was the ultimate professional. He could effortlessly glide between jovial banter one moment and then unambiguously draw our attention to the genuinely serious matters on the trip. It was all highly reassuring.

As the evening wore on and the group chat slowly subsided, we all started to drift off to our respective tents. By 21:15, despite the air temperature now down into single figures, Matt and myself were, in my opinion, 'butchly' stripped down to our underpants and cosily zipped up in our wonderful sleeping bags. I concede, Matt may have appeared the more 'butch'.

It really was quite nice to have some personal space away from the rest of the group; the sort that can only be achieved by sharing with someone you are totally at ease with or by being a solo traveller.

Matt and I chatted as we idly chilled-out. We agreed that both of us, following this long and eventful day, could have easily turned-in for the night well before the call for the evening meal. Following a long journey to reach Tanzania, precious little quality sleep over the previous 48 hours and an equatorial hike, we were both extremely tired.

Not surprisingly, though, because today had been so extraordinarily different to any other day I could ever recall, drifting off to sleep quickly was not a realistic option. The adrenaline and excitement were still coursing through our already over-stimulated senses. I think Andy and Mike were also in a similar frame of mind as we could hear them in their tent discussing favourite films, trying to wind themselves down.

Our chat, though, was far more varied, covering topics, such as, would we be changing underpants tomorrow? Had we taken our *Malarone* (malaria tablets)? And, what on Earth was Dougie doing on this trip? Because the tent 'walls' were not exactly soundproofed, we were very careful to lower our voices when discussing other members of the group. And, by the way, we decided not to change our pants. It simply wouldn't have been the 'butch' thing to do.

Following half an hour of mostly frivolous chit chat, I simply had to 'let one go'. It was met with an immediate 'reply' from Matt who, fair play to him, raised the stakes, much to our childish amusement. Remember: "If you're farting well, you're faring well." Oh so true and oh so funny.

After a brief bout of wind ping-pong in our tent, Andy and Mike joined in from theirs! To the four of us, it was hysterical but probably doesn't translate as such on the page of this book. It was a 'you had to be there' moment.

The next distinctive noises to be heard, and certainly not to be outdone by farting tourists, were the calls of the Colobus monkeys high up in the trees.

Having been brought up on the TV show *Tarzan* as a child, I knew what a monkey 'should' sound like. These annoying 'cheeky monkeys' certainly delivered on that (musical) score. It was initially a little disconcerting to be surrounded by this most unusual and very very loud aural activity as they called to each other but equally it was a wonderful, slightly primeval experience. OK, I was currently in a tent, in the dark, on completely the 'wrong' continent but I felt as though I'd stumbled into Sir Arthur Conan Doyle's *The Lost World*.

Sleep became hopelessly impossible. The visually vibrant daytime forest had now exploded into an audible night-life of inconsiderate, incessant chatter from 'party animals'... plus, my bladder was now fairly full.

As I realised no one was using our team toilet, I pulled on a fleece, worked my way into my trousers, now with the legs zipped on, zipped myself up, unzipped the tent and then realised I didn't have my headtorch. After much fumbling, and to Matt's obvious amusement, I eventually found it in my heap of belongings in the middle of the tent, stumbled out into the dark, chilly night air, zipped up our tent flaps, unzipped the toilet entrance, surveyed all before me (which wasn't a great deal), zipped up the toilet entrance and plonked myself down on the seat, unwilling to stand, ever so slightly panting and all zipped-out. Phew!

Eew... OMG (yep, taught to me by my kids) - the seat was wet! I hadn't noticed that. Clearly someone, presumably not the 'OK' ladies, had been careless with their aim.

I'd arrived in Tanzania armed with three bulky packs – yep, I'm a sucker for a '3 for 2' promotion - of wet wipes but hadn't, for one minute, expected that I'd need them for a pee; so, I didn't have them with me. Damn!

I did, there and then, whilst sitting in another person's urine, understand why ladies get so cross about the 'wet seat'. But, the damage was done. No point crying over spilt... um, pee. I resigned myself to the consolation of being reasonably comfortable within the confines of this blue, bijou canvas construction, roughly four feet square and six feet in height, surrounding a ground-hugging chemical toilet that ok, admittedly, had a wet seat.

After the return journey 'zipfest', I was back in my cosy sleeping bag and finally ready for some much-needed sleep. However, then it was Matt's turn. Following his fumbling and zipping and unzipping and zipping..., he was soon ensconced in the toilet tent. When he returned someone else from the group was tapped on the bladder by the call of nature. It was an incontinent's convention!

After half an hour, everyone had peed, some a couple of times, all human activity was relatively settled again and it seemed finally time to drift off to sleep. But this is a rain forest near the equator so something else decided to grab the limelight away from the bloody 'Hey hey we're the Monkees' gang. It started innocently enough when a creature at ground level, I would estimate of reptilian descent, croaked. It was quickly joined by its companion and soon a whole choir of them throatily performed a cappella. The slightly disturbing improvised cacophony then proceeded to be passed on like a baton relay as the noise encircled the camp in a Mexican wave of a calamitous, eerily fascinating, tropical symphony.

Once I'd determined that my life was not in any danger, I lay back and begrudgingly endured this latest novel experience from far outside my comfort zone. Rather than counting sheep, one might expect that counting frogs would help lead to sleep. But, it was pitch dark and it sounded as though there were thousands of them. Had they been there all along? Or did they all turn up en masse, at night time, to annoy campers? Would they consider attempting a tent break-in as an unruly mob in an amphibious assault and run amok? On that score, I felt sure they'd immediately turn around in disgust upon seeing the complete mess in our tent.

Eventually, as quickly as they had started, they stopped. Were they now departing the camp, like a touring troupe, or simply hanging around for their gig this time the following night? Thankfully, all was moderately quiet again.

There's always noise in a campsite though. Low-level chat, coughing and, in the UK, we might hear the hooting of an owl and almost certainly wind and rain. These are familiar sounds so it doesn't take too long for the brain to filter them out.

However, this was a rain forest, and almost everything was completely new to my senses. Consequently, my brain was working overtime to determine what sorts of animals might be responsible and which ones might be a threat.

I, once again, assured myself that there were no life-endangering creatures attached to the noises and attempted to relax. I was slightly annoyed that I hadn't been prepared for just how incredibly noisy a tropical jungle is at night! Honestly, if this behaviour was repeated in a campsite back home, there'd be evictions, ASBOs and scuffles breaking out. I even considered making a complete racket myself the following day, just as a means of spiteful revenge over these nocturnal nuisances. Yeah, let's see how you like it!

I desperately wanted sleep. It was getting personal now. I rolled over in a huff and then...

... the unmistakable sound of a snoring human being and this, trust me, was very high on the (sno)Richter scale, took to the Big Tree stage. The seismic disturbances of the deepest nose and throat bass notes could just about be felt through our sleeping mats. It was obviously a bloke, probably a large one, and, aside from laughing with resignation, Matt and I were so relieved he wasn't in our group and felt sorry for the poor soul who might be sharing with 'The Beast'.

I rolled over, again, convinced that it was surely, eventually my last meaningful movement before falling asleep. I should have known it wouldn't have been and little did I know that I was now only a few hours away from my dreadful *inaugural encounter* with that 'long-drop' toilet!

Chapter 6 – … Day 2 continued

… after reflecting upon my six-month journey which had led to me being in this slightly sorry state, and having rolled over more times than a hefty Double Gloucester cheese at the Cooper's Hill Cheese Rolling Festival in Gloucestershire, England, I decided that all attempts to sleep were futile.

That all too recent episode in the 'long-drop' toilet had not only come as a huge shock but it had now heightened my already heightened senses and I simply couldn't rid my mind of the sight of shite. So, resigned to no sleep at all, a final roll over onto my back, accompanied by a now obligatory huff, meant I was nicely in a comfortable position ready for my thoughts to process the previous day's events.

During this exercise, I decided to dream up (oh, for a dream) a scale of difficulty with which to evaluate each day's experiences. I was attempting to measure how Tough Or Easy the day had been and stumbled across, or maybe tripped over, the TOE index (see what I did there?). It seemed completely appropriate.

The hike that day had been tough for me during the particularly steeper sections of the forest track but, overall, not too strenuous. I had no headache or aching limbs. I decided upon a ranking scale of 1 to 10. 1 would be for an easy day featuring very little physical exertion with no aches or pains. I wasn't anticipating any 1s on this trip. 10, naturally, I reserved for the final push to the summit when I was expecting the most gruelling physical challenge of my life, together with the debilitating burdens of blisters, muscle fatigue and altitude sickness.

Feeling rather chuffed with my index, I awarded the previous day a TOE of 5. I decided not to go too high up the scale for fear of having to recalibrate later in the week when the going was expected to toughen up considerably. That decided, *maybe* I would get some sleep now?

People often claim that they had no sleep whatsoever after a restless night but it's quite possible I drifted off for a while, I really couldn't say.

Come the morning, at 06:00 to be precise, a cheerful, smiling face perfectly mirroring the quietly emerging daylight peered into our tent and asked us how we'd slept. I claimed to have had no sleep to which he replied, "That is normal." A small comfort, but one which I was happy to cherish as I felt sure he meant it.

Matt, too, had failed to hoard away any meaningful sleep but, at least, we'd both rested our muscles. This would be our one and only noisy forest camp so I felt assured that sleep would eventually be forthcoming, if only as a result of total exhaustion.

A subsequent question from our guide provided us with the luxury of placing an order for tea, coffee or *Milo*. It was so complicated at this time of the morning, following little or no sleep, to fully comprehend the question at first. Room Service in a tent in a forest camp part way up an extinct volcano was bafflingly incongruous.

Matt, sensing my hesitation or possibly confusion, ordered a tea for himself. Meanwhile, my thought process quickly rejected coffee on account of just one sip of the stuff at home causes me to wee for hours; weeing here had already caused me so much inconvenience and grief that I was keen to minimise that particular bodily function. Annoyingly, though, going without a mug of strong coffee a day did generally give me a withdrawal headache. But, hey, on this trip, headaches were inevitable so a 'lack of coffee' one probably wouldn't be traced back to its source. Ooh, so much to ponder?

I had no idea what 'Milo' was so sensibly didn't think this was the time or place to experiment. So, by default, it was another tea for our tent. I certainly hadn't expected 'room service' but it was a most agreeable, if slightly mentally taxing, early start to the day.

Matt and I, by this stage, had sat upright in our sleeping bags and were reflecting on our night. Our first ever night in an equatorial forest really had been a unique experience; literally an eye-opener as there had been precious little shut-eye. However, Matt, following a really lengthy yawn, stretch and fart, seemed completely unperturbed so I chose to join him in his 'unperturbity' and yawned, stretched and farted too. We were so in tune with each other. We were now partly prepared for the day's challenge and 'faring well'.

The disappointingly weak tea was, nonetheless, very well received as was the 'wash wash'; a bowl of hot water brought to the tent entrance with which to freshen up. What a splendid way to start the day. I wondered if Mrs Binout might consider this as part of a new morning routine back home.

The tea sparked my bladder into action and with the light now suitable for a game of cricket, I felt sufficiently confident to stroll a few feet into the forest to relieve myself up against a tree whilst being able to examine the surroundings for anything that might bite me, crawl all over me or eat me. Upon completion, I said 'sorry' and 'thank you' to the tree spirits. An incident-free wee - Hallelujah!

Ahead of breakfast, at 07:00, I cringed and shivered as I dressed myself in cold, slightly damp clothes. Matt, meanwhile, who has yet another middle name of 'I've done this before and here's a great tip for you', casually pulled some warm, dry clothing from the bottom of his sleeping bag then effortlessly eased into his attire for the day.

It was at this very instant that I noticed he was also wearing the smuggest of smug expressions, barely stifling a self-satisfied giggle! There was a moment of silence as time itself briefly held its breath. No words needed to be exchanged between the two of us as he basked in my returned expression of indignation.

From that day onwards, my 'clothes for tomorrow' have always been placed at the bottom of my sleeping bag the night before. I just wish the bugger had passed on that excellent tip a few hours earlier!

Only Steve was in the mess tent when Matt and I entered. Poor chap, he looked dreadful. Hollow eyes nearly falling from his drawn, harrowed face. He looked gaunt and exhausted. Understatement of the year, but I reckon he'd had a rough night. Had he been out all night on a bender with the 'party animals' or, more likely, were these visible symptoms of altitude sickness?

The three of us started comparing notes about the night before as we discussed all the various noisy distractions. Matt asked if Steve had heard all that stentorious snoring? And, as Steve placed his shaking head in his hands, hiding a resigned look on his face, the penny, or perhaps I should say shilling as we were in Tanzania, dropped.

Steve had, tragically, drawn the shortest straw in the Kilimanjaro Trek tent-sharing lottery. He was paired with 'The Beast', better known to us all as Dougie. Poor chap!

I instinctively dubbed him 'Unlucky Steve' as an aide memoire. He explained that he had tried sleeping, blocking his ears under his pillow and a few layers of fleeces, inside his sleeping bag, but to no avail. I wasn't at all surprised as Dougie's distressing night time noise pollution was way in excess, times six and squared to boot, of any snoring I had ever encountered; only finally surpassed by a portly walrus of a hiker in a remote mountain hut in Eastern Europe a few years later. Yes, *you*, if you're reading this!

As you might expect, yet another of Matt's other middle names is 'fully prepared'; his birth certificate reads like a novel. Consequently, he was able to very kindly offer Unlucky Steve a pair of earplugs for the remainder of the trip. The look of relief was blatantly perceptible on his wretched face.

The other bleary-eyed, sleep-deprived members of our motley crew gradually filtered into the mess tent. Sleep, or rather lack of, was the first topic of discussion. With Dougie not yet in the mess tent, Matt divulged, in hushed tones, the identity of the snorer. Shaking heads, rolling red bleary eyes and resigned tutting greeted this revelation.

Then, Dougie cheerfully breezed in with the air of someone who had experienced a blissfully good night's sleep. There was a slightly awkward silence as we all pondered how best to change the topic of conversation with only the subject of snoring currently on the agenda. A barbed, "Sleep alright Dougie?", maybe wouldn't have been the best approach.

Fortunately, we were soon presented with a mouth-watering breakfast, including bacon and porridge, which helped change everyone's immediate focus from sleep deprivation to stomach satisfaction. Everyone's utmost regard and respect for our chef rose steeply yet again; unlike our route ahead today I, for one, hoped... but, no. Have you seen the graphic on the next page?

Yesterday's trail had gained us 400 metres (1,320 feet) in altitude along a distance of only 5km (3 miles). It hadn't been too strenuous for the non-snoring members of the group. However, today's challenge seemed more demanding with a 719 metre (2,359 feet) gain in height along 8km (5 miles) of trekking. We had all day, though. Remember, it's not a race! Pole, Pole...

One of the more taxing challenges each morning, well, certainly for me, was the packing of my rucksack and kit bag. Rucksacks are carried by the individual hiker each day and should be packed with everything one might require for that day. They should contain items of clothing for all eventualities, namely waterproofs, two or three additional layers of fleeces, sun hut, woolly hat and gloves. If you're feeling pessimistic, then an extra pair of pants and socks wouldn't go amiss either.

Furthermore, 3-litres of water, your favourite snacks, sun protection and minor ailment remedies such as plasters, blister plasters, blister stick, throat lozenges, pain killers, *Imodium* or similar (to help counteract diarrhoea) etc are essential. Don't forget a camera and spare batteries. Everything else can be squeezed back into your kit bag, which the porters will carry to the next camp, and will be waiting for you, in a neat pile, upon your arrival.

We commenced shortly after 08:00. Our snake-like procession headed off through the forest. Not surprisingly, following the previous night from sleep-deprived hell before, I found it quite a struggle initially.

For my legs, this too was an experience like no other. This was the beginning of a second consecutive day of hiking in a most unfamiliar

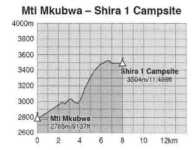

Mti Mkubwa – Shira 1 Campsite

environment both in terms of terrain and climate. It felt like my muscles, particularly those where the tops of the back of my legs met my lower buttock region (there's undoubtedly a more formal, anatomical name), were protesting against this early morning activity. They were incredibly stiff and emitted a strange sensation which provoked a wincing 'oooh arh' laughter pain, similar to the sensation of 'pins and needles', as opposed to an 'oooh arh bloody hell, this really hurts!' I'm sure they would have preferred a gentler reclining position with the luxury of an espresso and newspaper for an hour or so before setting off but, being *my* leg muscles, they reluctantly came with me.

Thankfully, with the varied distractions of yet another comfort-zone-free day, and the temperature quickly rising into double digits, I soon found an agreeable, albeit sweaty, rhythm and stripped down to just a single layer. Trousers, remained, most definitely, in 'zipped-on' long mode!

After only half an hour, the group had split into two sections: Dougie and everyone else. Probably no need to point out who was at the rear. This gap allowed the leading group to discuss the snorer in more detail. I just knew that everyone was secretly planning on grabbing a tent, at the next camp, as far away as possible from Dougie and, by unfortunate association, Steve.

I felt a bit sorry for Dougie, after all, he'd done absolutely nothing intentionally to completely and utterly ruin the sleep of his nine hiking chums, probably most of the support crew, possibly members of other parties at Big Tree Camp and, who knows, maybe neighbouring Kenya was affected too. To be fair though, snoring or no snoring, I'm not convinced anyone in our group would have enjoyed a good night's sleep anyway, such was *all* that incessant noisy nocturnal forest fauna shenanigans.

Our earthy path was narrow but very well defined. Even without a guide, I think it would have been impossible not to have successfully followed it, especially as it was enclosed on either side by thick green low-level undergrowth. In amongst this vegetation were dotted tall trees and lush shrubs of varying sizes and shades of green. So many greens! The canopy wasn't totally impenetrable though, allowing flashes of the blue African sky to vie for attention against the dominant verdant palette.

By mid-morning, we had been making slow but determined progress up the reasonably gentle incline through the forest and soon the lead group stopped for a break in a shady clearing. Everyone was in high spirits and coping well with the morning's hike; everyone, that is, except for me.

For the past hour, I have to admit that I'd struggled. During that time, I felt that my overriding aim was simply to keep up with group. I was no longer experiencing the sights and sounds. It had been a case of head down, keep plodding and don't lose contact with the youngsters. Not my best strategy. This effort resulted in me breathing far too heavily and sweating profusely like a... well, Dougie. It had been a struggle with no enjoyment whatsoever. Honestly, why oh why hadn't I heeded my own advice to go 'Pole, Pole'!

When Dougie eventually emerged into the clearing, with his personal guide Mekeke, I purposely joined him on a comfortable log. I was keen to have a 'getting to know you' chat and, to be brutally honest, sitting next to a fraught, perspiring wreck made me feel better about my own version of a fraught, perspiring wreck. The poor chap really was struggling and I almost, I stress almost, wanted to give him a hug. Had there also have been a giant slimy slug with cysts and halitosis slithering on this log, I know which I would have preferred to hug.

I discovered that Dougie was a seasoned campaigner having hiked all over the world, including to Everest Base Camp. Then, during one fleeting moment of exhausted reflection, he confessed to me that he wished he'd done more preparation for this trip and was "carrying 2-stone too much in weight". He was so candid. I could almost, I stress almost, have wept for him. He was such a lovely, down-to-earth, honest chap. The kind of man you'd be more than happy sharing a pint with in the local, whiling away the evening with genial chat about anything... except football.

Nevertheless, he was quite correct. To be frank, his stomach was almost the size of his 35-litre rucksack. He did seem nicely balanced though in a bulging symmetrical way. Viewed from above, he would have appeared as two circles combined in a Venn diagram.

There was no mention of a Mrs Doughnut or any mini doughnuts and, because he hadn't yet bonded with anyone in the group on account of him being thoroughly out of condition and therefore mostly hiking by himself, I felt myself hoping he had a good circle of friends back home. I'm sure he had. He was that kind of amiable easy-going chap.

After the break, the group soon split into three distinct sections: the younger fast ones; myself, now stubbornly but correctly deciding to walk at a pace I was comfortable with even if it resulted in me becoming Billy No Mates, and then Dougie and Mekeke bringing up the rear.

My new strategy really did make a huge difference to my well-being. Now I was avoiding being out of breath. My progress was far easier than it had been throughout the previous two days. I cannot stress highly enough just what a significant breakthrough this was. It no longer felt like a battle. I was able to appreciate the surroundings and myriad noises and shades of green of the rain forest: lush green, village green, grass green, moss green, pea green, putting green, and when the 'opportunity knocked' I'm sure I even spotted a 'hue of green'.

As I followed the path, I allowed my mind to follow its own unhindered trail of thoughts: What a bizarre day. I was seemingly on my own, traipsing through a forest in Africa with barely a care in the world. No emails to deal with, no phone calls to avoid, no school run to adhere to, no meals to prepare. Nothing. The structure and deadlines of 'normal' everyday life had been completely consigned to, for me, a welcoming bin of respite; carefree and cathartic. My only goal today was to get to the next camp. This living was liberating.

At pretty much 10,000 feet on the nose, we emerged from the forest zone bursting into a wide-open expanse of alpine heathland. Green and russet heather everywhere in fact. Slopes on our right-hand side stretched steeply upwards towards a ridge, while on the left, in the far distance, were the flat, dusty plains of Tanzania. All of this landscape was capped by a big blindingly blue African sky.

The air was so much fresher here. A slight breeze ensured a welcome cooling circulation of the warm, dry air. To my relief, the stagnant dense forest atmosphere had finally given way to a new Swiss alpine fragrance; the only things missing were lush green grassy mountain meadows - on account of total domination by all that heather - Heidi, Julie Andrews, some singing nuns and an annoying yodelling herdsman.

Matt was patiently waiting for me so we enjoyed the magnificent vista together. As far as the eye could see, it was apparent that the trail would now exclusively follow this new, predominantly green and russet heathery landscape. Consequently, I declared the rest of the day a bitey-thing-free-zone, zipped off the bottom of my trousers, bared my legs and rolled my sleeves up; exactly as I would for a stroll along the Cornish coastline on a sunny June afternoon.

I'm a decade older than Matt but, on this trip, he adopted the role of 'older brother'. He enquired as to my well-being and was pleased to hear that I was in fine fettle. There was no need for me to reciprocate; he was definitely fine. Matt was in his element. He's happiest when outdoors but these past two days had even exceeded anything he'd experienced back home. The childlike glint in his sparkling brown eyes portrayed a man excitedly at one with his environment. Maybe we should have then held hands. Then again... maybe not.

At this point, aided by a little bit of squinting, it was possible to see other groups way up ahead on the distant steep slopes gradually weaving their way towards the horizon like colourful beads on a thread. They did look a worryingly long distance away but I reminded myself "It's not a race!" We had more than enough time to reach Shira 1 Camp.

We were now officially in what is called a low alpine zone (heathland and moorland) and the vegetation, that I recognised, was dominated by the heathers. Totally! If Matt and I had conceived a daughter at this moment, we'd have christened her Heather.

For now, though, I craved a purple geranium. These weren't the ordinary knee-high heathers that I had in my flower beds at home. Some of these specimens were far taller than me and, unimaginatively in my opinion, are known as 'giant heathers' or *Erica arborea*

OK, I didn't see any geraniums but every now and then, in amongst these heathery giants, stunningly vibrant bright blood red, buttercup yellow and juicy Seville orange flowers were dotted around the green canvas. It was as though a giant tube of *Smarties* (minus the much-maligned blue ones) had been sprinkled over the landscape. All in all, it was a welcome contrast from the ever-increasingly monotonous fifty shades of green forest environment we had just left behind.

Lunch was due to be enjoyed in a delightful spot high up on the slopes and overlooking the scorched, flat plains. As Matt and myself approached the already-settled members of the group, in my eagerness to sit down and join them, I carelessly tripped. Instinctively, I reached out with my left hand to break the fall. Unfortunately, my palm found a protruding root and was punctured by its uncompromising stiff woody stem.

Naturally, being a direct descendant of the legendary Black Knight, I dismissed it as a mere 'flesh wound'. Asim, however, had other ideas and came rushing down to inspect. He then hailed Vincent, one of our assistant guides, who quickly joined us with a comprehensive medical kit.

A nervous smile failed to disguise my genuine dread. My only thought now was, 'Please don't produce a syringe!' He didn't - oh, such relief - and in no time at all Vincent had cleaned the bleeding wound, covered it in what might be described as a 'Donald Trump toned' orange spray, put a plaster on, and neatly finished it off with a generous bandage wound around my palm through the gap between thumb and forefinger and, for good measure, partly around my wrist too. It was a magnificent dressing and made me feel rough, tough and ever so brave. As is my way, I even considered a limp for maximum effect and sympathy.

I hadn't fully appreciated it, but it's always most important to view cuts, no matter how minor, as a serious matter. This sentiment was fully enforced as I witnessed Vincent's alacrity and fastidiousness in dealing with my unfortunate mishap. We were in an unforgiving environment in which hygiene was scarce and infection lurked around every heather. I was now neatly trussed up, back in the game and even received a smidgeon of short-lived sympathy from the group which I casually waved aside - with my bandaged hand, naturally. Gosh, I was also possibly inching closer to becoming Matt's equal in the 'Rugged Outdoorsman' department too. Butch, brave and now approaching 'rugged'. Yep, I was getting there!

Eating my packed lunch in the warm sunshine with a view to die or trip up for was a wonderful opportunity to appreciate the surroundings in restful, peaceful observation. We quietly tucked into the sandwiches, boiled eggs and fruit, that is, until the reverent silence was shattered by a sweaty, grunting creature heading up the trail towards us.

It was, of course, Dougie and his now unofficially appointed personal guide, Mekeke, and, amazingly he'd also managed to acquire his own porter who was carrying his rucksack. "How *does* he do it?" I thought. It was almost as though Dougie was on separate trip to the rest of us.

He finally re-joined his official group and was presented with his packed lunch into which he dripped copious amounts of sweat - let's call it 'dressing'. Did he care? Nope.

It was during lunch when I discovered that Andy and Simon were both suffering quite badly with headaches and nausea. They were young, fit lads but had clearly been hiking far too quickly. I seemed to recall, possibly in Henry's book, that this 20- and 30-something male age group were particularly prone to altitude sickness simply because, to be blunt, their egos wouldn't permit them to go 'Pole, Pole'. Asim had already given them both some aspirin.

Bugger, why hadn't I thought of bringing any aspirin? Back in 2007, due to an awkward and stressful alignment of circumstances, I'd had to pay a visit to hospital in order to have my heart monitored. It was there that I'd learned how aspirin thins the blood. Apropos of that, one of the human body's ways of dealing with a lack of oxygen (an effect that notoriously increases with altitude) is to produce more red blood cells which, in turn, thickens the blood and can lead to headaches and, sometimes, worse. I'd come armed with half *Boots the Chemist's* stock of paracetamol in my bag and now it seemed somewhat redundant.

I spoke to Asim about this and he confirmed that, in his long experience of high-altitude environments, aspirin was indeed the best drug of choice. Fortunately, he assured me, he had plenty to go around should the need arise. Please note, aspirin is not suitable for everyone though.

It's worth mentioning that Matt and myself had also brought along with us tablets of the 'high altitude wonder drug', *Diamox*, with us as a back-up. Whenever you read about Kilimanjaro, it's never too long before the subject of *Diamox* is discussed. The jury used to be out on this one, not because it's illegal, in which case I suppose the jury would be sitting in, but whether or not it's effective.

Certainly, it's the first course of treatment in bad cases of altitude sickness. For those who choose to bring it with them, it's either used, hopefully, as a cure for mountain sickness or as a prevention; taking it prophylactically, to give the correct medical terminology.

We'd bought ours back in the Spring, from a dodgy dealer in a nightclub - only kidding - and took half a tablet each whilst hiking in the Brecons in order to find out whether we might react badly in some way to this new medication. Fortunately, neither of us noticed any ill side-effects at all, sadly not even the ability to speak Welsh. Everyone is different, though, and it is most important to seek professional advice on this particular subject.

When lunch was over, it was obvious that I was in high spirits and feeling fully fit. Both Andy and Simon asked if they could walk behind me, effectively nominating me as a pace-setter. What a boost to my confidence that was. I'd never been higher than the ground I was currently standing on. These two whippets had been to South America, high regions in the Himalayas and the like, and they wanted to follow *me*!

Resisting the temptation to fist-pump and shout something along the lines of, 'Back of the net!' I casually said 'Yes, of course'. I was now the leader, yes leader, of a splinter group of three. Not only that, I was sporting a bandage too. What a hero! I remembered not to limp as we set off towards our next goal - the summit of the final ridge.

As the gradient eventually flattened out, we began to bear right and then... there it was! As the eye meandered across the expansive Shira plateau before us, the dominating and ever so slightly menacing presence of Kibo was beckoning in all of its magnificence.

At that moment, Kibo was partly shrouded in cloud but, by looking at the shape of the formation on either side, it was possible to imagine what the very top might look like.

In my mind's eye it all looked fairly straightforward and, filling in the clouded middle section, I pictured a nice gentle stroll to the top on a constant, not impossibly steep, gradient. But then the cloud parted!

Crickey! I hadn't seen that coming. I was aghast at the actual vision of the snow-clad cone and true summit with its rather alarmingly steep 'sides'; it was not the moment to attempt to recall the proper geological feature's terminology. 'Sides' sufficed for now. It was a leviathan of truly biblical proportions barely diluted by the fact that it was still several miles away!

I was, truthfully, very concerned and what breath I had had was whisked away in an instant. I was surely not worthy. I almost felt compelled to kneel down and worship at this Volcanic God's feet. But, that would have appeared cowardly and not particularly macho, and in direct contrast to the ever so brave explorer with the beautifully bandaged life-threatening wound. So, I stood there gaping in awe and farted instead.

This was a suitable resting spot, so we all plonked ourselves down upon a rocky outcrop, fumbled on some snacks and cautiously evaluated the challenge in front of us, attempting not to portray any signs of genuine concern. I say "all", in actual fact it was nine members of our group plus Asim and the assistant guides. Dougie, naturally, was nowhere to be seen. I was confident that he and his loyal support team of two were indeed still in Africa, perhaps later to be discovered by an explorer muttering the immortal words, "Doughnut Dougie, I presume?"

My attention was diverted by three cheeky striped mice which scurried between our feet, presumably attracted by the possibility of fallen crumbs. It was tantalisingly tempting to hold out a hand offering food but to be bitten by a wild animal, no matter how small or cute-looking, was not worth the risk part way up a mountain and would, no doubt, have required another bandage - possibly a 'needle moment'! One bandage was bad luck and sympathy-inducing. Two would have made me look reckless, or clumsy, possibly both.

A group of American-sounding hikers soon walked past. Maybe a dozen, ranging in age from 27 up to mid-sixties, I would have thought. They all sounded in high spirits as they chatted and laughed amongst themselves.

We all said "Hi" as they wandered by, with the pleasantries being whole-heartedly reciprocated. Everyone is simply part of one big, like-minded team on this mountain.

And then, near the rear of their group, were two (in my opinion) very attractive ladies; possibly twins. Despite my flirty hormones having been raised, I barely took any notice of them. Yes, they both had long blonde hair tied in pony tails which flopped gently over their rucksacks, wore brown Craghoppers-branded shorts with back pockets, ankle-high hiking boots with socks pulled up to the beginning of their Californian-tanned calf muscles, were 27-years-old and therefore in exactly the same 27-49 demographic age group as myself ensuring we'd have a great deal in common, but other than that, I have no recollection of the pair at all.

Within seconds of them being out of earshot, Matt remarked upon how I'd pathetically waved to them with my heavily bandaged hand on full display in a blatant attempt for sympathy and attention. He may have had a point. The ladies, disappointingly, hadn't appeared remotely interested in my potentially life-threatening wound, which was sad as it would have been an ideal ice-breaker; they probably thought I was a right accident-prone nob. Asim found this all highly amusing. I blamed the altitude.

At 3,536 metres (11,601 feet), this resting spot was comfortably (and uncomfortably) the highest I'd been on foot before and was, in fact, today's high mark along the route. From here, Asim was able to point out that night's camp, Shira 1, low down on the vast plain and seemingly not too far away; it appeared to be a gentle descent of only 20 minutes or so. Clearly, the hard part was well and truly behind us.

An uplifting sense of mission accomplished... for now. Asim was also able to point out the following day's camp, suitably named Shira 2. That camp was just beyond this gently rising plateau, in the direction of the looming Kibo, and in amongst some higher ground populated with boulders, rocks and patchy vegetation. Tomorrow didn't appear too challenging at all; not too far away and the steepness of the terrain appeared completely manageable. I relaxed a bit.

By the time we reached Shira 1 Camp, the porters had already erected all the tents! Matt, one of the first to arrive, had secured one quite a distance away from Steve who, presumably, would be joined by Dougie at some stage later in the day.

Upon spreading out in our tent, Matt discovered that there was a huge rock under what would have been his head position when he lay down. It would have made it impossible to rest, let alone sleep.

I half-heartedly offered to take his side of the tent but discovered that he hadn't been whinging about a mere ant hill of a rock. This was seriously hard core.

Of course, at this altitude, it was also hilarious; we soon called Asim over to see for himself. He was hugely apologetic that the porters had pitched the tent so inconveniently but joined in with the overall amusement. We asked if we could be moved to the American camp right next to the blonde twins.

Instead, after Asim called a couple of porters over, we were repositioned *only* ten feet to one side. We made sure it was ten feet further away from Dougie's pitch though.

Matt and I collected our 70-litre kit bags, neatly deposited in a 'group' pile by the porters and then crawled inside our tent. We were now settled in Shira 1 Camp at 3,504 metres (11,496 feet, or eight-and-a-quarter WBs), not the highest I'd ever been on foot before (that had been accomplished only twenty minutes ago) but certainly the highest I'd ever camped at.

As was now the norm, I removed everything from my 35-litre rucksack and stacked it haphazardly in with the pile of the contents of my kit bag, which I'd already evacuated into a semi-neat heap. So, 110 litres of my 'stuff' peered back at me from the floor of our tent as if to say, "Now what?"

Well, that was quite easy. Most of my 'stuff' was still contained within 'stuff sacks'. These sacks are a wonderful way with which to compress the more forgiving 'stuff', eg clothes and soft comforting bears, into a smaller, more compact space allowing one to cram even more 'stuff' into a kit bag or ruck sack. Not surprisingly, they are also known as 'compression bags'. They will not compress harder 'stuff' such as cameras, mobile phones, medication and kitchen sinks.

Because I had absolutely no idea what was contained within each stuff sack, I emptied the contents of each and every one, forming a significantly larger, not-so-neat heap. This was becoming my preferred, if slightly random, means of being able to locate anything.

Matt considered it a disgraceful mess but, in jovial spirits, accepted it was 'my way' of camping at altitude. In hindsight, I should have labelled each stuff sack with a list of its contents.

In complete contrast, Matt had formed an impressively neat arrangement of his 'stuff' and had already filled a rather useful 'interior tent pocket' with his headtorch and toiletries. I immediately followed suit, pretending not to follow suit.

A loud puffing, heavy panting, painful grunting commotion soon announced the arrival of Dougie and his team into camp. His slightly chaotic, raucous arrival was accompanied by dry throaty coughing and globular mucoid spitting. I must admit, he didn't look at all well. Once again, he was dripping in sweat and his cheeks bore the deep red shade of a vintage claret. This was only the second day. I was convinced he'd never make it to the top. To be fair, though, his 'man melons' were still performing in perfect unison.

That afternoon we were offered the opportunity of a "15-minute" acclimatisation walk. My research, yes another very useful snippet from it, had described the significant benefit of these hikes; it's the classic high-altitude mantra of 'climb high, sleep low'. If offered, then one should certainly jump, or shuffle slowly, at the chance of such a walk.

The simple premise is that acclimatisation is aided by sleeping at a lower altitude than the highest point attained in any one day. So, on this trek, an acclimatisation walk would take us to a location a few hundred feet higher than the day's camp, where we would sit around chatting for half an hour acclimatising before returning down to camp for the evening meal and eventual night's sleep. Sleep! If only!

I didn't expect Dougie to join us but Simon also remained at camp. His tent-partner, Robert, explained, in great detail, that Simon was feeling pretty awful, suffering from nausea and a particularly bad headache.

I then noticed Robert's rather impressive piece of photographic equipment. I'd recently been bought a similar DSLR camera as a present from Mrs Binout but hadn't brought it with me due to space and weight constraints. I was quite pleased, though, with the progress that I'd made in learning how to use it so asked Robert all about his, hoping to pick up one or two useful tips. That was a mistake! Robert went on and on and on and on, so long in fact, that I developed a Pavlovian reflex action to nod mutely in appreciation at regular intervals whilst thinking of ways to escape.

And so, 'Boring Bob' appropriately became his moniker (for mine and Matt's purposes only). In fact, Bob was so boring that in a previous life he would have been a laminated occasional table.

Mekeke was the leader for this very pleasant afternoon jaunt and was very possibly ecstatic at having been separated from Dougie. No wonder he displayed the smile of someone about to embark upon a personal 'long walk to freedom', albeit for only "15 minutes."

He explained we were heading off in the general direction of Shira Cathedral, an impressive towering feature of lava on the Shira Plateau. It would be the highlight of tomorrow's hike up to Shira 2 camp.

Perhaps it was because the group was already suffering with two early casualties of altitude sickness that we walked at a noticeably slow pace, even by my standards. Reading about the effects of altitude is one thing, actually *seeing* the effects, though, most definitely focuses the mind on the potential dangers. So, 'Pole, Pole' it was. It suited me fine.

We eventually stopped at a huge boulder which a couple of the young lads climbed, of course. Such was the incline, I didn't feel at all inclined to join them. I was happy enough just to admire this huge lump of rock against a reddening backdrop of the upper slopes of Kilimanjaro. It was a beautifully tranquil terminus for all eight members who had joined in that afternoon.

We enjoyed the changing hue of the low-lying clouds, which had formed around the base of Kibo, from pure pearl white to soot grey, as the sun began its gently descending navigational path across the sky.

Throughout this whole trip, our visual senses would be constantly treated to a spectacular spectrum from Nature's own palette. In particular, it was the rocky landscape of Kilimanjaro that would display many moods of mesmerising colours. Depending on the weather conditions and time of day, it could threaten with dark sinister blacks, haunt with ghostly silver greys and warm with earthy shades of rust and amber, all of which hinted of its explosive volcanic past. To me, it gave the mountain a being, a spirituality. I fully appreciated why, around the world, so many mountains and volcanoes, and their incumbent spirits, are revered and worshipped by the locals.

In a world of my own, Boring Bob caught me by surprise as he sank himself down beside me. His desire to continue talking about cameras was as obvious as it was worrying. Fortunately, I was able to quickly change the subject and discovered that he worked in IT - bugger, I should have stuck with camera talk. I personally think IT people are twenty-first century versions of train-spotters. At least railway 'anoraks' are easy to spot, loitering by themselves at the very end of railway platforms, armed with flasks, snacks, an HB pencil with eraser, and dog-eared A4 or A5 notepads, bursting full of numbers and text written in their own special 'code'. These people do keep themselves to themselves and, I'm informed, are perfectly harmless.

IT folk, however, are impossible to distinguish from normal people. They think in meta data and their own code; characteristics which are not overtly obvious. They reside in IT Departments and perform 'fixes' in the dead of night, so no one is sure what their true population is. They reluctantly lurk in dark corners at office parties, stutter uncomfortably at the sight of skirt, are often very dull, and don't do irony. Bob was no different. When talking *at* me, Bob hadn't stuttered once, a reasonable indication that I hadn't put my skirt on for the acclimatisation walk.

Thankfully, Mekeke soon decided that we should return to camp. It provided me with the perfect opportunity to pretend to have a most urgent question for Matt, thereby freeing myself from Boring Bob's vapid clutches. By the time we arrived back in camp, the acclimatisation walk had indulged us for a largely enjoyable hour and a half. So much for the advertised "fifteen minutes". Maybe Mekeke had simply over-indulged himself in his quality time *away* from Dougie.

Back in our tent, flaps open, Matt and I enjoyed a tranquil sunset and quietly witnessed the landscape colours gently pass through their fascinating transformation from deep rusty browns to the cooler icier greys.

As Shira plateau tucked itself up in a cold black volcanic blanket, Kibo performed one final show of earthy orange brilliance before it too succumbed to a dark dormant state silhouetted against a sky that then quickly transformed from white, through every shade of blue before a rich velvety black finale. Was there ever a grander end to a day? I couldn't recall one.

Of course, it was only the end of daylight hours. We still had an evening meal to feast upon.

Soon the group had convened in the mess tent when something quite strange happened. We were all happily chatting away when Dougie grunted in, stood stock still, looked around, let rip an enormous fart, and then walked out again.

There was a bewildered silence as we all thought, "Did he really just do that?" It took a few moments of slightly awkward private deliberation, as everyone mentally grappled with what had probably just happened, before Matt bravely confronted the elephant in the room and opened up the most recent incident to a group discussion.

"Maybe this was normal behaviour for Dougie?" We doubted it though. With recently acquired superficial knowledge of these conditions, we all blamed the effects of altitude. The general consensus was that Dougie was possibly now struggling mentally as well as physically. He was all too obviously farting well but he wasn't faring well. Poor Dougie.

The evening meal, once again, was an incredibly masterful culinary experience. The highlights were the soup followed by chicken and vegetables.

The eight fit members of our team were all in high spirits, chatting away, sharing jovial banter punctuated with lashings of laughter.

However, Dougie was not his usual perky self and poor Simon didn't say a word. He did look ghostly pale, hardly ate anything and soon headed off to his tent, (unnecessarily) apologising for leaving the group so early that evening. Hopefully a good night's sleep would sort him out we all wished. Ahead of him turning in, Asim, who had been keeping a watchful and caring eye over Simon administered a further dose of aspirin to him.

At the end of the meal, Asim addressed the group. He checked how we all were in a combined, loving motherly fatherly way then introduced Vincent who would explain tomorrow's route and plans on the way to Shira 2.

I thought about nudging Dougie with a "Shearer, Shearer" (a well-known chant by Newcastle United fans when Alan Shearer played for the team) but with him not being into football (yes, I still couldn't believe it) it probably wasn't worth it. Besides, I still had that little regional joke lined up ready to trot out, given the right moment. It contained no references to football so Dougie would surely get it and it might even cause him to roll around with laughter... which, in hindsight, might be a dangerous state to be in given his recent 'outburst'.

Vincent informed us that during the following day we would initially head across Shira Plateau towards the 'Cathedral' which we would then climb. From its base to the top of this volcanic feature, it would provide us with a gain of 200 metres (650 feet) then dropping down by roughly 100 metres before a steady climb up to Shira 2 Camp. The 'Cathedral' would not only provide a very useful acclimatisation hike but also a wonderful viewing platform with which to appreciate to whole of the Shira plateau.

On each subsequent evening, we were given a similar briefing with, firstly, Asim asking about our welfare and fielding any questions from the group. Then one of the assistant guides would talk us through the next day's agenda. Not only was this a most informative briefing for the group but it was also part of the development of the assistant guides on their own personal career journey to becoming a head guide. A perfect opportunity for them to practice their English-speaking skills too.

Having returned to our tent, as might have been expected, despite now feeling physically weary, sleep didn't naturally follow. So, after chatting about the day's events, Matt and I commenced a lively farting competition much to our childish enjoyment. However, these were those terrible eggy farts, the ones with that awful hydrogen sulphide odour, which have a habit of lingering for quite some time and staining walls. Not exactly ideal for a shared tent but it kept us amused. We eventually traced the origin of these farts back to the boiled eggs contained within our lunchtime picnics.

The laughter spread to Andy and Mike 'next door' and they soon joined in with the farting. Wow, this was such great schoolboy fun. I considered Matt to be the winner of our windy duel but eventually, as tiredness prevailed, the jovial banter, the giggling and the farting all began to subside. Not long afterwards, though, the snoring began!

I pondered that day's TOE index. Despite one or two strenuous stretches of terrain, it hadn't been too taxing for me, the landscapes had been exhilarating at times, and I had no headache. So, it was a rather pleasant 6 out of 10.

Chapter 7 – Day 3. Shira, Shira

In the night there had been a rather beastly sound of a boar with inflamed bronchial tubes and a blocked snout in the search of tasty truffles. Neither Matt nor myself were overly concerned. The hog-like sound had followed a welcome break in the snoring.

As the grunting and growling had given way to phlegmy coughing, the unmistakable sound of a zip was heard. There was further coughing, punctuated by the odd flabby fart, before the team toilet tent was unzipped and the beast disappeared inside leaving us to giggle between ourselves; perhaps other team members were chuckling away too.

Fifteen minutes later, Dougie was once again tucked up like a generous Northumberland sausage in a Yorkshire pudding duvet and blissfully snoring away. Poor Steve. I hoped his newly acquired earplugs were stifling the seismic activity in their tent.

The morning began with our orders for hot drinks just as the daylight was gently unfurling. Our 'room service' weak teas soon arrived together with the 'wash wash'.

The previous evening, I had witnessed a stirring end to daylight. This was now, arguably, surpassed when we tied back the flaps of our tent to reveal an astounding daybreak. The coarse volcanic dust on the ground was twinkling with a silvery frost and crunched like fresh snow under the weight of booted footsteps. Our red plastic 'wash wash' bowls glowed like translucent wine gums and the steam from the hot water rose gently into the freezing air against the dull grey silhouette of Kibo and a pale barely-blue cloudless sky. Shadows were slowly shortening and the gentle low orange sun lit up the broad white smiles of effervescent porters. The lime green section of our tent glowed with an ethereal luminosity as though it had been decorated with highlighter pen graffiti. There was not a sparrow's breath of wind. Matt and I sat in silence and absorbed this astonishing birth of a new day.

Soon, the chatter and frenzied activities of the porters brought us back down to Earth. And, with great pride and a nod to Matt's sage advice, I was able to dress myself in warm, dry clothing admiringly retrieved from the nether reaches of my sleeping bag. As a newly established 'seasoned hiker', it was now surely only a matter of time before my stripes would be awarded to me; possibly even at breakfast. What a cracking start to the day.

At breakfast, there was no awards ceremony. A tad disappointing, it has to be said. However, Asim was keen to discover whether everyone was well and how we'd all slept. Most of us discretely looked across at Steve, exactly as we had done the previous morning at Big Tree Camp. It was all too clear that his night had not been great, yet again.

For the second consecutive morning, he appeared gaunt with the disposition of someone who'd had little, if any, sleep. Which, of course, was exactly the case. Conversely, his tent-mate, Dougie, was pleased to announce that he'd enjoyed a good night's sleep despite his headache. Yep, it was the classic case of Snorer's Law: the most unfair universal law that, while leaving behind in its wake a trail of bleary-eyed devastation, a snorer will always sleep well.

The real problem, however, lay with Simon who once again looked particularly limp, lifeless and lousy. He was slumped in his chair like a miserable fat caterpillar suffering with depression. Despite being dressed in several layers of thick clothing including a woolly hat and gloves, he was still cold, with an odd shiver now and again teasing his delicate frame. What we could see of his expression, was distant and pale, and his eyes were flat and emotionless. He only managed to pick at his breakfast preferring instead to cup, with both hands, a mug of tea for comfort. He didn't speak a word. Asim handed him a couple of aspirin tablets which he struggled to swallow with water. It appeared as though his body was reluctant to eat or drink anything at all.

Not only that, but it had been decided that Simon would be taking, presumably extremely slowly, an older-established direct route up to Shira 2 campsite today. This old trail provides a steady incline and is approximately two-thirds of the length of the route that the rest of the group would be taking.

Simon was to be accompanied by Asim, not be expected to carry a rucksack, and would have all day in which to complete his four-mile journey of endurance.

For the rest of us, today would pose a hike of 10km (just over 6 miles) and a gain of 391 metres (1,283 feet) in altitude. We would be faced with the additional exertion required to climb the 'Cathedral'.

Around 08:00, the nine of us, together with assistant guides, headed off across the relatively flat Shira Plateau towards the first destination of the day, namely Shira Cathedral. With the temperature hovering just above freezing now, it was a chilly start. However, the air was still and the sun had begun its generous daily warming routine. So, the immediate dress code was long trousers and one fleece over a rapidly-ripening two-day-old t-shirt. Fortunately, any stale body odour was efficiently diluted in the fresh morning air.

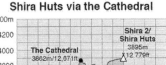

Shira 1 Campsite – Shira 2/ Shira Huts via the Cathedral

The gentle walk retraced our acclimatisation route from the previous afternoon across a dusty landscape strewn with rocks and boulders of varying sizes, from small stones to weighty giants the size of double-decker buses. Upon arriving at the huge boulder, the 'lads' had previously climbed, we headed off to the right and directly towards the 'Cathedral'.

From here it was clear to see that this formation rose sharply like a sheer wall of dark grey rock and was fairly flat at the top, rather similar in appearance to a mini version of Table Mountain, in South Africa. A deepening blue sky with a huge white cloud rising from behind the

'Cathedral', provided a perfect backdrop. I wondered what indeed lay behind this dominating structure?

We crossed what appeared to be a shallow dried river bed, evidence of the significant presence of water at some stage in the past. It was approximately 20-feet wide, bordered by gently rising banks on either side. Within the river bed itself, resided tufty, hardy grasses. We all reclined on the far bank, as one might do on a pebbly seaside beach, feasted on some early-morning snacks and basked in the glorious sunshine. It was the perfect opportunity to zip-off my trouser legs, remove my fleece and await the sound of the ice-cream van.

There was indeed soon a distinct sound. Our ninth member, Dougie, who had separated from the main group soon after departing camp, arrived with the chuffing bluster of a steam train struggling up a steep gradient. The ever-smiling, ever-cheerful, ever-loyal Mekeke was carrying his rucksack.

Dougie was greeted with smiles and genuine affection all round. Every day, he just kept going and going. In his own team; in his own world; most of the time. The warmth of the group towards him triggered a huge smile across Dougie's sweaty face as he plonked himself down in a puff of rancid BO, with a sense of triumph and relief. It would have appeared awfully rude to have edged away from Dougie, so we all remained in situ but turned our heads to breathe.

I'd developed a bit of a 'hot-spot' on my right big toe, so removed my boot and sock and applied a generous coating of 'preventative' smearing from my 'blister stick'.

I'd discovered 'blister sticks' during our training hikes in the Brecons. It's a bit like a lipstick-sized deodorant stick. The idea is to smudge some over the area of skin upon which it feels as though a blister might be developing. It had always worked for me and, I'm sure, had prevented many blisters from forming. Matt had also been equally impressed with its healing properties and had brought along a blister stick too. I doubted that he'd need to use it though. His feet had always appeared completely immune to blisters.

I opened up a general discussion on blisters amongst the group. Not one of them had any blister concerns. I presumed, as seasoned hikers, their feet were as tough as their old boots. Mine were clearly of a softer disposition but I had every confidence in my blister stick.

Having rested and with Dougie, once again, part of the main team we next headed to the base of the 'Cathedral' where we removed our rucksacks and prepared ourselves for the 200-metre (650 feet) ascent.

It was from here that I could fully appreciate this huge buttress of rock surrounded by steep 'spires' and pinnacles which, with a large breath of imagination, could indeed resemble a church-like place of worship.

There was a significant mist rising up from behind the 'Cathedral' so we all departed carrying waterproof tops. The route up was over hard volcanic rock, loose scree in parts, with small tufts of hardy grass sprinkled haphazardly over the terrain. The scree sections led to a degree of scrambling as hands and, occasionally, knees were also employed in the climb. Yes, ungainly at times but a hugely enjoyable break from trudging 'Pole, Pole' across a gently rising landscape.

Higher up, we passed a few blackened, leafless trees which appeared dead, draped in bearded lichen adding to an eerie sense of desiccation in the ghostly mist that had suddenly engulfed us. This much cooler, moist air prompted everyone to pull on their waterproof tops. The temperature had dropped quickly by five degrees or so; not cold, merely a stark, rapid contrast.

Soon, there was a section where I could finally see what lay on the other side of this lump of rock. Peering through fleeting breaks in the mist, it was possible to catch glimpses of a dramatic, almost vertical drop of at least a thousand feet, maybe two, possibly three - I didn't want to think about it too much. Crikey, I hadn't anticipated that! I'd made the incorrect assumption that 'the other side' would have mirrored our far friendlier approach with its gradient that would be forgiving in the event of a slip or fall, and certainly not leading to instant death.

Despite my terrifying ever-constant urge to jump off high places, I was compelled to stand at the edge of this craggy viewpoint and fight my instinct. My firmly rooted-to-the-spot legs shook more than was ever witnessed at a Shakin' Stevens concert.

It's all possibly a bit weird but I do know other people, admittedly not many, well, two if I'm honest, who have a similar urge. It does give me a truly petrifying thrill both in the 'there and then' as well as replaying it in my mind later on, making me squirm in grimacing abject horror.

Peeping tentatively over this precipitous edge, I could see a verdant landscape in the misty abyss below. It was from out of these depths that the mist was rising from, before wrapping us in its damp swirling embrace.

As quickly as the horrifying view had revealed itself, the curtains of cloud then closed leaving me oblivious once again to the oblivion below.

At this point, Matt appreciated that I was mentally in a safe place and asked me to take a few photos of him standing right close to the edge, smiling, and without a hint of fear. He kindly reciprocated but I positioned myself six feet away from the drop zone, forced a fake smile and displayed an air of, "will you hurry up and just take the bloody photo!"

Obligatory photos thankfully over, it was then a relatively straightforward scramble, lasting fifteen minutes, to the misty top of the 'Cathedral' where we were greeted by a 4-foot high cairn; instantly provoking thoughts of the man-made piles of small rocks on the mountains at home. I wasn't sure whether cairns were just a 'British thing' but it was nice to acquaint ourselves with this 'home comfort'. With a dramatic drop, swirling mist and stunning views I could have been stood at the top of the magnificent mountain of Cadair Idris in Snowdonia.

From the 'Cathedral' summit, it was like looking across the top of a baked rock-strewn steak and kidney pie and we were standing precariously upon a small remaining piece of the protruding crusty pastry edge. One stumble in the wrong direction and we'd be on the baking tray and quite probably toast… or crumbs.

We all enjoyed the mandatory group photograph at the 'Cathedral's' peak as well as, after much jovial jockeying and playful elbowing, one or two individual shots. There was a palpable sense of achievement that we'd bagged this modest summit. It really was wonderful to have Dougie with us as a proper part of the group but this was still tempered by heartfelt concern for Simon. He was missing out on this minor highlight and was no doubt struggling simply to put one foot in front of the other. At the top of this buttress of a 'Cathedral' we, perhaps, should have said some prayers for him.

This had been an exhilarating acclimatisation excursion and, at 3,862 metres (12,671 feet), the highest I had ever been on foot. I was racking up personal bests on a daily basis now. In fact, I hadn't had such a good run of PBs since playing *Daley Thompson's Decathlon* on my 48K ZX Spectrum back in 1984.

On the way down, we passed a group of three American ladies, which included the blonde twins. This was a great chance to strike up a conversation and develop a rapport so, pointing to the top, obviously with my bandaged hand and remembering not to limp, I informed them there was a Costa Coffee at the peak.

For a split second, there was a look of disbelief before they fully appreciated what I'd said. It produced a smattering of giggling. I was definitely 'in there'. Matt, however, quickly deflated any delusionary egotistical thoughts by suggesting that they were laughing *at* me. As I clung on to *my* version of events, I conceded eventually that he may, yet again, have had a point. We never encountered the twins again; maybe they were playing hard to get.

Once down and off the 'Cathedral', we collected our rucksacks and turned 'rightish' towards Shira 2 Camp. Usually my sense of direction is very good but, on this mountain, I really struggled during large parts of the day, from mid-morning to mid-afternoon, with our orientation. I think the problem lay in the fact that at this equatorial latitude the sun was, quite often, perpendicular overhead in the sky. Back in England, the sun is rarely directly above and sensing its whereabouts usually points to a general southerly direction. And so, on Kilimanjaro, I became the first ever explorer to discover the fickle, fifth point of the compass: North, South, East, West and Feck Knows.

The route now headed upwards, steeply in places. It was noticeable that the vegetation was now predominantly hardy, low-level sorry-looking scrub. Most was green, some were grey with silvery tips at the end of woody stems and occasionally there were flashes of small citrus lemon flowers successfully grabbing the admiration of hikers. The landscape was largely rocky and dusty like a set of a science fiction film. The larger rocks and boulders were decorated with ancient scruffy white and rusty orange lichens, as they had been for hundreds, if not thousands, of years.

Ever-present now was the looming ice-capped monster: Kibo. We were heading straight towards it but it would still be four days before our attempt at the summit. Tantalisingly in view but strictly 'out of bounds' until the acclimatisation process had been fully completed. It was like a childhood memory of having to keep hands out of the sweetie jar.

Shortly before the route began its final steeper ascent into camp, we encountered a helipad which had been 'constructed' on a flat piece of sandy, dusty ground cleared of any vegetation or other impediments. In the middle was a large 'H' neatly 'spelled-out' using small yellow and white stones, surrounded by a matching yellow and white circle, large enough to accommodate a helicopter. A sorry-looking limp, torn and generally weather-bedraggled orange windsock on a pole completed the site's features. The helipad was adjacent to the end of an official park track, suitable for 4x4 vehicular access.

Nearby, there was a bit of a commotion interspersed with concerned silences from a group of hikers and guides gathered around an emergency vehicle sporting several red crosses on the grimy white bodywork.

The 'ambulance' soon trundled off along the track leaving a plume of dust as it headed down towards the Londorossi Gate on its way out of the national park and on, presumably, to the nearest hospital, leaving behind the small group of hikers and guides we could see.

I found myself standing next to a lady (she wasn't my type so I had no reason to show off my bandage) and I enquired as to what had happened.

Mary explained that the person in the 4x4 was her sister, Liz, who was suffering from a form of acute mountain sickness (AMS).

AMS is generally divided into three categories: mild, moderate and severe. This particularly unpleasant and potentially dangerous side effect is an issue that anyone who is considering tackling Kilimanjaro or, for that matter, any climbs at high altitude, is made fully aware of in any pre-trip research.

The problems occur due to air pressure dropping as altitude increases. At the very top of Kilimanjaro, the air pressure is only 40% of the level experienced at sea level, so there is a real struggle to force a 'normal' amount of oxygen into the body.

Such was my interest, as well as concern, that I'd become a walking medical encyclopaedia on the subject. Being a rock'n'roll binge-drinker, I knew I could cope with the mild form; symptoms merely being nausea, a thumping headache and, generally, feeling crap. Nothing new there; just the usual Saturday, Sunday and Monday morning feeling for me.

With the moderate form, the rather bad headache cannot be shifted by standard painkillers, the nausea will lead to puking everywhere, and the feeling of crap moves up the scale to 'shite'. Without any actual experience 'in the field', I had already unprofessionally diagnosed Dougie with 'mild' and Simon with 'moderate'.

A severe case, however, will lead to all sorts of incapacitating characteristics, which will include a lack of coordination, mental confusion, and an inability to stay awake (rather like a typical Friday girls' night out in Newcastle - I jest).

There is plenty more on the topic if you care to research the subject further where you will inevitably stumble across the highly alarming pair: HACO (High Altitude Cerebral Oedema) and HAPO (High Altitude Pulmonary Oedema) which appear to have the Grim Reaper on speed dial; assuming there's a mobile signal.

Liz's AMS had reached the severe level at which point there is only one course of action: descend *immediately* and as *quickly* as possible. There is no arguing, *whatsoever*, with the head guide. Your trip is *over* and you are taken off the mountain and into hospital.

Mary was clearly concerned, as well as, in no small measure, shocked. I got the feeling she was keen to talk a bit longer. I was happy to remain and listen.

Prior to their trip, Mary and Liz hadn't discussed this particular scenario. So, within a short space of time they had had to agree upon whether Mary should continue with the trip or not. Liz, naturally, was insistent that her sister should carry on up the mountain and, with a heavy heart, that's exactly what Mary had decided to do.

It won't surprise you in the least to learn that I'd read about this type of dilemma in my research. When two or more close friends or family members are on the same trip, it's very important to have a mountain 'pre-nuptial' agreement in place. Matt and myself had agreed that, should one of us have to descend, then the other would definitely continue. No debate.

Tackling Kilimanjaro had been a major investment in both time away from work and more importantly our families, as well as money. Consequently, nothing, other than a life-threatening illness or death, was going to prevent either one of us from continuing.

In the eventuality of one of us having to pull-out, we concluded in our 'pre-nup' that the other one would summit on behalf of both of us; unless it was me being rushed to hospital, in which case I'd insist upon Matt holding my hand in the ambulance.

And so, the two sisters had arrived at a similar conclusion albeit in hasty and unforeseen circumstances. Their trek had only started the previous day when they had all been *driven* up to Shira 1 Camp, thereby losing at least a day's acclimatisation hiking on the mountain and effectively immediately being 'dumped' at eleven-and-a-half thousand feet; a shorter, cheaper route up the mountain. Little wonder Liz was so ill.

I certainly didn't mention that we, on the other hand, had chosen the route with the longest period of time spent on the ascent that we could afford; I somewhat smugly thought it though.

It had reassured me greatly that, despite the obvious increase in cost, the extra day or so we had paid for would be crucial to improving our chances of standing at Uhuru Peak. OK, two of our group *were* already struggling but I reminded myself that the Doughnut simply hadn't prepared at all and Simon had started off far too quickly.

I said goodbye to Mary, wishing her and her sister the very best of luck, and proceeded towards the next camp.

After a short steep scramble over some rocks and boulders, we arrived at Shira 2 to find our five tents erected very closely together; only a couple of feet between each one. It gave the appearance of an attractive green and purple dayglo terraced street but, of course, there would now be precious little respite from the anticipated snoring. Matt

117

knowingly rolled his eyes at me, laughed and selected our tent for the night. It didn't really matter which one for none of us would be immune to the Beast. We would all suffer tonight.

Initially, though, I was simply delighted to have arrived at 3,895 metres (12,779 feet, or a fraction over nine WBs); the highest I'd ever been on foot. Yep, another PB in the bag! And, for those with even a rudimentary grasp of Maths, we were exactly *only* 2,000 metres from the summit. That, to me, gave the impression of a task much easier to contend with than its imperial equivalent of six-and-a-half thousand feet.

This camp had a large single-storey building with the now familiar green corrugated pitched roof. It was of sufficient size to house the ranger's office and a modest toilet block.

Nearby, was an official-looking, fenced off area roughly half the size of a tennis court. It contained a communications aerial of thirty feet in height and what looked like a small weather station.

The fifty or so tents that were at this camp were all dotted amongst rocks, boulders with the only vegetation being green heathery waist-high shrubs.

Our tents had been positioned in a seemingly quiet yet slightly removed location on the edge of camp. Was this on account of Dougie's snoring? It did seriously cross my mind. I estimated a somewhat 'challenging' distance of thirty yards from our tent to the toilet block; roughly a day's hike at this altitude.

This whole camp was on a slight gradient and our tents were no different; cue, time for another useful 'snippet': I recalled, from Stedders' (on account of constant referral to his publication during this trip, I felt I was growing closer to Henry Stedman on a daily basis and he therefore now warranted a nickname to reflect our manly bond that he is, admittedly, unaware of) book, that under such circumstances your head must be higher than your feet or you would risk a very bad headache indeed. Oh, those ubiquitous headaches!

This heady altitude was now beginning to take effect on our group's ability to be sensible when it came to the administrative tasks. An example of this was patently demonstrated when we stumbled into the ranger's office to complete our sign-in 'stuff'.

Boring Bob, yes, Boring Bob the IT chap, suddenly threw off his inhibitions and nerdy shackles. Under 'Occupation', he signed-in as a 'Tattoo Artist'. Boring Bob had morphed into Robert the Rebellious!

The snowball effect was immediate and our group suddenly boasted: a 'Porn Star', a 'Gay Porn Star', a 'Bush Trimmer' and, given the previous entries, a possibly dubious sounding 'Facial Expert'. Someone had written: 'Dead'. Hmm, how all very childish! I won't confess as to who signed in as what; 'What goes on the mountain, stays on the mountain'.

To huge amusement and satisfaction, we'd scored a victory over the Red Tape oppressors; all led by Rob the Rebel. Perhaps I'd been wrong about Bob. Maybe, in his previous life, he'd been a laminated occasional table *and* some matching flat-packed comfy chairs.

From the elevated location of our camp we had a perfect view of the vast sprawling Shira Plateau that now lay behind. The impressive 'Cathedral' geological formation was clearly visible, along with its steep 'rear' side and alarming drop, as was the dull orange 4x4 track now silhouetted against the grey scrubland.

It was also just possible to discern our previous camp, four miles away in the distance. To our left and right was a continuation of the sloping rocky terrain we were camping on and behind us was the unmistakable presence of Kibo.

In the foreground, the inimitable shape and sounds of Dougie were also quite apparent. He was grunting, panting, coughing, swiping sweat from his brow and his moobs were swaying hypnotically in a beautifully choreographed fashion as he staggered from side to side towards camp. So, all appeared completely 'normal'. As I witnessed him struggle, I couldn't help but genuinely admire his undoubted tenacity.

Simon and Asim were also visible, maybe half an hour behind Dougie. That was a measure of their exceptionally slow progress today.

Mekeke once again led the afternoon acclimatisation walk and, on this occasion, we headed steeply up over a rocky incline in the general direction of Kibo. By the time we'd stopped to rest, I would guess, we'd gained a very useful two hundred feet or so in altitude. Neither Dougie nor Simon elected to join us.

As we chilled out high above camp, I attempted to send a text home but, perhaps not surprisingly, there was no signal. Mekeke was seated next to me on a rock and, rather oddly, asked what mobile service provider I used. I won't advertise their name in this publication as I'm still waiting for a reply to a complaint letter I sent them four years ago. Judging by what I've read online, I can only presume they have a huge backlog to clear. Anyway, I'll give them one more year and if I've not heard back, I shall move to a competitor; no doubt, equally as incompetent. (I did and they were)

On answering Mekeke, he knowingly pointed to a boulder approximately twenty yards away and when I stood on it I was rewarded with a mobile signal! Incredible! I'd have been less surprised if Dougie had come bounding up to meet us carrying his own rucksack and wearing only a jockstrap and matching sports bra.

However, and I wasn't aware of this at the time, I hadn't unticked an option somewhere in 'Settings' so was immediately buried in an avalanche of incoming emails. Stupid smart phone user.

One of them had been sent by a most engaging gentleman, who is nowadays very well-known, offering to give me £10,000,000 in exchange for all my personal details. It appeared to be a reasonable offer. Also, he was conveniently close by too, on the same continent, in

Nigeria. I felt torn but ultimately resisted replying to his most generous proposal.

Two subsequent emails also caught my attention but I chose not to place an order for some blue tablets which were on special offer and would keep me 'going all night' - to be honest, all I wanted was a good night's sleep - or for a miracle male enhancement product. I pretended to delete both but had secretly kept them in order to forward to 'a friend' upon my return home.

Back down at camp, I was pleased to sense, at long last, some bowel movement and went in search of the camp 'long-drop' toilets. I hadn't yet 'been' on the mountain. My most recent 'movement' had been back in our lodge whilst being closely monitored by that persistent gecko.

When it comes to this particular activity, I'm usually as regular as clockwork; 08:10 every morning, since you ask. I normally take a newspaper with me, to read from back to front of course, and enjoy a peaceful sit down for, well, as long as it takes really, sometimes a good half an hour.

I prefer not to rush such events hence I chose not to over-occupy our team toilet tent. And, it has to be said, my thoughtfulness was rewarded by finding a 'long-drop' with a wooden seat structure giving the impression of a proper loo. Not only that, it was reasonably clean.

Nonetheless, I gave it a comprehensive wipe-down with my biodegradables, took off my marigolds and sat down to enjoy some quiet relief.

A few soggy thuds announced my business was going well. I even considered counting, as one does with lightening to estimate its distance away, how long it took from 'release' to landing on the pit floor in an attempt to calculate the length of drop. The frivolous effects of altitude once again at play.

Sauntering back to our tents, I met a most-engaging American chap, by the name of Jim. He was greying and, most likely, in his early sixties. We

121

chatted for quite some time. He, his wife and daughter were tackling Kilimanjaro as a long-standing family ambition and had booked a safari trip afterwards. He knew England quite well, having been stationed at RAF Upper Heyford for several years. We were, therefore, able to discuss both cricket and football, although unbelievably he'd never heard of West Bromwich Albion; I attempted to provide him with a potted history. His call of nature - or was it the 'potted history'? - and me becoming quite cold in the rapidly cooling air, prompted us to part, wishing each other the very best of luck.

Simon chose not to attend the evening meal but Dougie crawled into the mess tent. Being very much a no-nonsense type of bloke, he claimed to be feeling "OK". However, his now usual 'I'm about to have a coronary episode' red rustic face was unusually ashen and he wasn't his normal chatty self.

Yet again, it was a most enjoyable feast: onion soup to begin with, followed by meat balls, potatoes and green beans with a lovely vegetable sauce, all finished off with pancakes. The only thing missing was a brandy and cigars. A postprandial gentlemanly game of billiards would not have been feasible on this slope though.

Yet again, I awarded our chef a Michelin star. I never did discover his name but he was an expert at cooking for us 'Hairy Hikers'. Which neatly reminds me, that North East-based joke...

Following the hearty meal, I decided to try the *Milo* which Mike had happily been enjoying every day. He passed me the carton and upon reading the label, I discovered it was a chocolaty drink for "future champions".

Having worked in marketing myself I knew that the aim was to sell things to consumers that they didn't really need by preying on concerns and fears whilst also making an outrageous profit - is that not the definition of 'marketing'?

My snide cynicism, however, was superseded by my desire to make the metamorphosis into a 'future champion' in a high-altitude environment. And actually, it really was rather delicious and uplifting. In fact, my cocoa-induced high spirits coupled with Dougie now looking like something from *Zombie Mountain Monster Moob Snorers III* finally prompted my North East-based joke. So, during a lull in conversation I said, "Hey Dougie, I heard there was a nasty crash involving a truck load of tortoises just outside Newcastle. Police say it's a turtle disaster."

There was an ever so brief silence, perhaps everyone was attempting to decipher my very poor attempt at a Geordie accent, and then, thankfully, much laughter. It visibly tickled Dougie too but in his delicate state he was desperately trying to maintain bodily control for fear of a trouser accident. As I've said though, high altitude is the perfect venue for comedians, even rubbish ones.

Next on the agenda was the briefing for the following day's route. Naturally, I'd researched each day's itinerary before departing for Tanzania but that was 'on paper'. This was in the field... on the mountain.

It's not until you're actually on the trip when you alarmingly discover each day's challenge has usually been made just that little bit more testing by the added impediments of: lack of sleep, loss of appetite, headaches, nausea, AMS, and crappy 'crap-traps'.

Still, it could have been worse... um, nope, not sure it could actually. As a consequence, Day 4 sounded rather daunting: an initial, at times, steep ascent of 732 metres (2,405 feet) up to the 'Lava Tower' followed by an, at times, steep descent of 641 metres (2,103 feet) into Barranco Huts camp. "At times" was worryingly undefined.

If the challenging elevation gained and subsequent loss wasn't bad enough, the high point of the route stood at 4,627 metres (15,180 feet). I knew this would really test exactly how acclimatised we'd all become and maybe, just maybe, AMS would be lurking somewhere along the way.

123

Interestingly, and slightly disappointingly, it meant we would be camping tomorrow at only 91 metres (298 feet) higher than tonight. Tomorrow really would follow the classic mountain mantra of 'climb high, sleep low'.

The total distance covered, though, of 10km (just over 6 miles) would be pretty much the same as today, so that was a small mercy. Certainly, Joshua, the assistant guide who explained the route, didn't appear at all perturbed. Mind you, on the compass point indicator of laid-backness, *all* the guides tended towards an east-to-west orientation of chilled.

Once back in the comfort of our tent, any detail about tomorrow's route was soon forgotten as we embarked upon the customary windy bottom frolics (that surely has to be an isolated hamlet in Devon?).

Because the tents were so closely positioned together any such noises were easily heard amongst the group. As expected, Andy and Mike soon entered the unofficial competition and it wasn't too long before Karen and Olivia joined in.

I've always considered farting to be very much a male preoccupation. Blokes seem to find the activity really amusing especially after a few pints or, on occasion, at altitude. A perfect one should be quite flamboyant and odourless. But, I do concede, that a grossly bad-smelling expulsion does have a time and a place; preferably not in a too confined space.

One of my all-time heroes is in fact a professional flatulist; the French performance artist, Joseph Pujol, whose stage name was 'Le Petomane' (roughly translating as 'the maniac farter' or 'the fartiste').

His career in theatres began in 1887 and he would thrill audiences by, amongst other things, 'playing' tunes, performing 'fart impressions' and blowing out candles from a distance with a well-aimed fart.

At his peak, he was the most well-known and highest paid entertainer in the whole of France.

He eventually died in 1945, aged eighty-eight, after which there were many requests by medical schools to examine his bottom region but his family declined (maybe they couldn't be arsed to sign the paperwork?). The wonderfully gifted Leonard Rossiter played Pujol in the 1979 short film, *Le Petomane*.

Honestly, Karen's kick-arse performance had been absolutely brilliant, plucked from the top drawer of skid-marked underwear. And, with all inhibitions literally blown away, she was comfortably tonight's winner. Huge respect.

As the amusement subsided, so Dougie's snoring began to dominate the audible spectrum. It's possible that Steve was deriving some comfort in all of us having to intimately share in his own regular night time torture.

If the US government ever wanted to extract information from someone, say, for example, dressed in an all-in-one orange suit, then they'd only need to threaten them with a night in a tent with our Dougie. Actually, maybe a chat on DSLR cameras with Boring Bob might work too?

Up until now I'd been, whilst not exactly happy, tolerant of the effort and disruption involved in popping outside in the wee hours to do just that. It involved fumbling around for the headtorch, putting several layers of clothing on as well as socks and footwear and reluctantly leaving the cosy warmth of the sleeping bag, not to mention stepping out into the freezing night air. Now, at almost 13,000 feet, it really was far too cold to be venturing outside after sunset, even more so at 01:00 in the morning with the temperature a few degrees below zero.

Whilst listening to Dougie's reverberations, I'd been pondering this dilemma for a few hours and eventually came up with a master plan.

So, once the call of nature duly knocked on my bladder's door, I advised Matt that I might be making a bit of a commotion. He was intrigued but I didn't reveal my plan until I'd found my plastic sports water bottle.

Unlike my aluminium 1-litre bottle this one, with the top removed, had a wide neck, of sufficient diameter to easily insert part of one's manhood; preferably mine. "Inspired!", I thought to myself.

You won't be surprised to learn that, yes, during some research I'd discovered 'she-wees' – portable, handy-sized female urinal devices. How clever and convenient, and now I'd created a 'he-wee' of my own.

I immediately felt at one with Bear Grylls who usually manages to fashion a two-storey shelter, comprising of kitchen area, en suite bedroom, study, and living room with a fireplace out of some moss, jungle creepers, large leaves and a tarantula's scrotal sack and have a wee at the same time. We were clearly hewn from the same adventurers' rucksack of instinctive ingenuity.

I then positioned myself into a kneeling position and attempted to find my 'chap' which, due to the cold, had retreated in an attempt to stay warm. I warned Matt that any minute now I'd be peeing into my bottle. With an air of indifference and a slight chuckle he wished me, "good luck with that, mate."

As any bloke will tell you, it's quite challenging having a pee with an audience so I struggled to overcome the ever-increasing sense of expectancy in our intimate tent. All that was missing was a drum roll... oh, and a gecko.

Eventually, a bit of banter - along the lines of, "get a bloody move on will you, the suspense is killing me!" - relieved the tension, unlocking my bladder, and I filled the bottle with what looked like a rather appealing very strong hot steaming tea. The dark colour prompted me to gulp down half a litre of water... and so, the relentless, endless cycle of drinking plenty and weeing loads would be maintained ad infinitum or, at least, until I'd conquered the mountain.

However, I was rewarded not only with simply curling up inside my sleeping bag with minimum effort but I also now had the most unlikely hot 'water' bottle.

I made a note in my notebook to tell my mate-in-waiting, Bear, once I was home (I have since read, much to my disappointment, that these wee-fed 'hot water bottles' are not uncommon amongst high altitude hikers. I hadn't been as innovative as I'd thought). That probably explains why Bear didn't write back.

Today had, once again, been a relatively easy hike with the thrill of Shira Cathedral and I wasn't suffering from any ailments. I gave the TOE index a pleasant 6 out of 10.

Peace and contentment at last. *It* then started snoring again... but I did 'enjoy' my best sleep of the trip so far. Mind you, nights one and two hadn't exactly provided any meaningful competition.

Chapter 8 – Day 4. A bit of a brute

With the dawn light beginning to weakly illuminate the tent, I blearily woke up with a nasty little nagging headache. Bugger! I instinctively reached for my aluminium water bottle and inadvertently knelt on the plastic version causing an explosion of cold 'tea' to erupt. Bollocks! There was momentary pandemonium as I quickly ripped my sleeping bag away from the rapidly forming pool of pee with most of it now running down the sleeping mat towards the bottom of the tent. It might have been a freezing cold frosty morning. I didn't know. I certainly didn't care! Within a matter of a few seconds I was outside, in my grundies, carrying both sleeping bag and mat and placing them on a nearby rock hoping that the rising sun would soon be able to commence a drying-out process.

Panic over, my 'washing' haphazardly hung out to dry, I stood proudly in my underpants and daps, fleetingly admiring my instinctive handiwork in response to, what could have been a 'turtle disaster'. The freezing cold frosty morning then bit hard and I promptly scurried back into our tent.

Naturally, I received no sympathy whatsoever from Matt but after discovering that the residual pee hadn't penetrated any of my other belongings, I joined in with the banter. I then forced the best part of a litre of water into my system and took two paracetamol in an attempt to arrest my headache. The arrival of weak tea and 'wash wash' signalled a less stressful and more orderly start to the day.

At breakfast, the usual, 'How did everyone sleep?' topic of conversation was replaced by 'Teepee, 'tea pee' Tentgate'. I quite basked in the headlines as, indeed, my sleeping bag and mat were hopefully basking in the drying sunshine. The last thing I wanted that evening was to have to snuggle into a damp bag with it reeking of a high street shop doorway on a Saturday night. At least it was my own urine though, so that was something.

Following breakfast, we all departed en masse at 08:00. On the far edge of the camp, having only been hiking for two or three minutes, we encountered a quaint little wooden rectangular-shaped structure. Quite simply, it was four pieces of timber, each approximately six feet high and spaced four feet apart in a square formation, upon which was a green corrugated iron, pitched roof. Under this roof, was housed a small wooden box, like a nesting box, with a convenient slit into which pieces of paper could be 'posted'.

In front of this was displayed a sign: 'Tourists Suggestion Box'. [I just know that the Editor will be itching to add an apostrophe onto the end of 'Tourists'. She's like that; all the bloody time, in fact. But, that's how it was written - just let it go]

Naturally, our group was unable to let this opportunity go either. Despite not having even warmed up yet, we all stopped for a couple of minutes and pondered: flushing toilets, showers, a café, a pharmacy, a massage parlour, and a separate part of camp – a mile away – reserved for snorers. It was, of course, all very highly amusing.

Soon after leaving camp, a three-way split in the group developed.

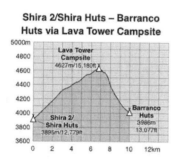

Shira 2/Shira Huts – Barranco Huts via Lava Tower Campsite

Dougie was in his own three-man team, Simon was walking very slowly with Asim by his side carrying his rucksack, and the rest of us were making steady progress up a reasonably challenging rocky inline towards today's alarmingly highpoint at the Lava Tower.

This section of the route gained a daunting 732 metres (2,405 feet) in altitude, taking us up to 4,627 metres (15,180 feet), assuming we got there.

The Lava Tower itself is a huge, striking lump of rock, standing alone and, if climbed, will add 57 metres (190 feet) in height-gained to your trek.

Thankfully, as with the rest of the fit members of the team, I was physically fine. No blisters or muscle aches and pains. However, I really did notice a difference in my breathing now. I was taking much longer, deeper breaths in order to feed my body with its required levels of oxygen. I was also walking more slowly than at any time on the trip to date and, annoyingly, my headache was showing no signs of abating.

There was now very little vegetation on display. Instead, huge boulders were strewn over a rocky landscape. Our path meandered, avoiding the boulders and the, seemingly, constant incline was occasionally interrupted by random undulations and folds of the terrain.

As the morning developed, the steep, gruelling nature of the climb saw our leading group becoming further and further spread out with me bringing up the rear now suffering with a very nasty headache. It was a dull dense pain around the back of my head bringing with it a slight queasy feeling of nausea. I instinctively increased my intake of water. Noticing that I wasn't my usual cheerful self, Matt slowed down to join me for moral support. I was really grateful for his jovial and encouraging company.

We were now two and half hours into the trek. A cold dank mist then descended, prompting the adding of a couple of fleecy layers plus a waterproof jacket.

For the first time on the trip: I was feeling cold during the sunlight hours and I experienced a lowering of my spirits. It wasn't a freezing cold sensation, more a damp one which chilled the flesh of my torso. Of course, having a bad headache didn't help matters either. And, within a few minutes, I'd stopped to locate my fleecy gloves and place them on my cold fingers.

I knew a moment such as this would arrive sooner or later, confirming the physical challenge had now been joined by the mental test. I anticipated that it was simply the hors d'oeuvres before the main course of horrors would be served up the closer we got to summiting; possibly with a surprise side dish of 'delights' that were not on the menu but had been mischievously devised by the high-altitude mountain maître d'.

None of these culinary-based thoughts made me the slightest bit hungry. However, I did force myself to consume another half a litre of water and then trudged on with Matt by my side. As usual, he was cruising along, barely out of second gear.

Soon, due to a mixture of the vast fluid intake and cooler conditions, the call of nature inevitably came knocking. I spied a suitable large boulder and walked around to the rear only to find a rucksack flung on the ground and a sorry-looking chap leaning against the hard rock in a squatting position with diarrhoea streaming out of his backside. His palms were steadfastly gripping the tops of his thighs, assisting him in maintaining his awkward position. A grimace betrayed the strain he was enduring. On first, and only hurried impression, he appeared to be a well-kitted out hiker with a large part of it currently around his ankles; some of which was now being decoratively splattered.

He was obviously in great discomfort and I felt that a friendly, chirpy, "Hi, how's it going?", would not have been appropriate. Best left as a one-sided brief encounter I thought. Like a mountain leopard, albeit one with a sore head, I stealthily crept away in search of another suitable location. I don't think he had even noticed me. Poor bloke! It was an unsavoury reminder that there's always someone worse off on this mountain.

Following a little over four hours of ascent, mostly in silence, Matt and I arrived at the Lava Tower meeting up with the six members of the group who had been ahead of us.

Andy was leaning over a rock adopting a familiar pose which suggested he was about to be sick. Feeling in a similar state, I decided to join him at 'Puke Boulder'; not on any maps. We compared ailments and like two hunched-over shady drug dealers, decided to crack open Andy's stash of aspirin and optimistically wash them down with an excess of water.

We weren't up to jovial craic but we'd laughed in the face of adversity, poked it in the eye, tweaked its moustache, plucked its eyebrows, and managed to persuade the contents of our stomachs to remain in situ; similar to our unrelenting headaches, which were stubbornly squatting inside our heads resisting eviction notices.

This resting point allowed time to fully admire the imposing dark volcanic structure of the Lava Tower which, perhaps not surprisingly, no one felt inclined to climb.

At 4,627 metres (15,180 feet, very nearly eleven WBs) - yes, you've guessed it - it was the highest I'd ever been on foot. However, feeling fatigued and suffering from that nasty headache, I didn't feel a huge sense of achievement but, instead, was overcome with a feeling of terrified awe at the massive rockface of Kibo that completely dominated the scenery behind us. It was a foreboding obdurate wall of dark rock, rising sharply hundreds of feet above us, which deadened the ambient sounds as a black hole might devour light.

We were now standing at the western edge of Kibo and, as any crow bird-brained enough to attempt a straight line of flight from here would tell you, we weren't that far from Uhuru Peak itself; maybe as little as two or three miles.

It was an up close and personal encounter with what appeared to be an impossibly steep rockface. I presumed, by the time we'd trekked around to the south eastern point of Kibo, where our final summit path would begin, the route would be kinder on the eye... and legs, for that matter. Fortunately, that was another two-and-a-half days' off yet thereby, hopefully, allowing plenty of time to get myself back into peak physical and mental condition, and shake off any inconvenient altitude sickness.

Additionally, I took comfort in the fact that we were currently standing at only 35 metres (115 feet) lower than our final camp before the actual summit attempt. That meant we barely had to climb any higher before the 'final push' to the top. I was, therefore, filled with, admittedly, slightly hopeful confidence, in a wishful-thinking sort of way, that my headache would have eased by then as I'd be fully acclimatised.

Of immediate concern, though, was the two thousand feet of descent that now lay ahead of us in order to reach our next camp, Barranco Huts. This would perfectly demonstrate that the Lemosho Route is not uphill all the way.

I think I'm similar to lots of people who genuinely struggle with some aspects of long downhill treks. They place strain on a different set of muscles than the 'uphill' ones, push the knee joints to breaking point and also present a new centre of gravity to contend with.

My research (yep, I know) had prompted me to buy two pairs of cheap, telescopic walking poles specifically for the potentially strenuous downhill sections of this point and the return journey down from the summit. I'd clearly planned for a successful outcome. Well, fail to plan and all that!

I'd given one pair of poles to Matt as a pre-trip gift. He'd seemed genuinely impressed and really thankful, leaving me a little embarrassed as they *really* were very cheap indeed. I felt now was the ideal time to proudly release these downhill saviours from my rucksack and eagerly took hold of one with much excitement.

However, I was soon awkwardly fumbling around, firstly trying to extend my pole and then twist-locking it secure. At least I'd already removed the cardboard backing and those notoriously impossible-to-undo plastic ties (other than with an industrial diamond-tipped cutting tool) before I'd left home.

Matt, naturally, had no such problems. An effortless tug followed by a wristy twist, a smug grin and he was ready. He'd earned himself the right to a beautifully performed self-satisfied eyebrow-raise too. He took full advantage.

Hmm, 'Matt the Mechanic Maestro' sprang to mind but, as I'd known him for years, so most of the time could actually remember his real name, giving *him* a catchy nickname was pointless really. Mind you, just at that moment, 'Matt the Smug Bastard' wouldn't have gone amiss.

And so, seeing me faff and struggle and blaspheme to the Mountain Gods, it was left to 'Matt the Smug Bastard' to ensure I had a long firm extension... well, we were intimate tent mates now.

Time for that tricky descent!

I followed 'Smuggo' down a very steep, rocky section at the far side of the Lava Tower, our proud poles poised to penetrate any accommodating crevice or cranny.

It wasn't long before a cross between a starched stiff stick insect and a ponderous praying mantis following a heavy night out on the tiles (had I mentioned my headache?) was lurching from one pole to the other in *the* most ungainly exhibition of mountain descent; possibly, ever.

I couldn't believe how tricky it was to use the damn poles. Everyone else I'd ever watched using poles seemed to glide perfectly co-ordinated down a ravine whilst chatting away making it all look ridiculously effortlessly easy. So, I begrudgingly persevered in the hope that it would surely only be a short matter of time before I too had mastered the art. The praying mantis lurched on in good faith.

An hour later, I threw the blasted sticks down in semi-mock disgust and stamped on them. So too did Matt. It quickly developed into a brutal and frenzied attack on the four defenceless poles; one of mine possibly damaged beyond repair. In hindsight, I think we went a step too far.

We both agreed that we were simply not going to get on with these useless, not fit-for-purpose devices. Had I kept the receipt? We glared in disgust at the pathetic scrap metal heap that lay before us. It was complete, utter, random carnage of garbage; worthy of the Turner prize.

That was the first and last time that either of us has ever used walking poles. But, it was the poles who laughed last and loudest. Naturally, we couldn't leave them there. So, after Matt had retracted three of them, the remaining one being too buckled to shorten, we strapped them with a vengeance to our rucksacks and effectively gave the buggers a free ride down to camp.

It was somewhere along this route that I first noticed the most peculiar tree groundsels or, for keen botanists, *Dendrosenecio kilimanjari subsp. cottonii* (yes, I looked that up). I wasn't in the best of moods by this stage and it was now quite damp and misty again, similar to my trouser environment.

However, Matt and I chose to stop for a more detailed look at this strange flora. They appeared to be as a curious concoction of a pineapple, a palm tree and a cactus, standing anywhere between six and twenty feet tall. Each had a single scabby umber coloured 'trunk', with the texture of a scorched pineapple, eventually 'branching out' into three or four 'limbs' with large green spiky leaves, the size of swords, with yellow flowers forming a crest on the tips. I'm sure experts, especially those who refer to them by their Latin name, will have a much more accurate description than I have managed to recall.

They were slightly unnerving in that they were top-heavy giving the appearance of a dangerous spiky Medieval Mace which might swoop violently at any moment and impale into your head. Oooh, a headache cure maybe?

It may have been my current state of mind but I sensed they were part plant, part fiend. Their looming presence in the swirling mist suggested they might creep up on you when your back was turned, wrap their spiky limbs around you and absorb their prey through some lengthy gruesome, excruciatingly painful digestive process. If John Wyndham hadn't already written *The Day of the Triffids,* I could easily have penned it there and then... but it would have been titled *The Day of the Dendrosenecio kilimanjari subsp. cottonii.* Admittedly, the title not being as catchy as John's book. Thankfully, though, we were armed and dangerous ourselves with three 'good' poles between us, in case of a surprise ambush by these menacing shrubs.

Once some common sense had prevailed, Matt and I gingerly approached these herbaceous horrors. We stood next to them, touched them and then, satisfying ourselves that they wouldn't devour us, we took some 'intimate' touristy photos with them... and survived.

Unfortunately, the silent party pooper that was altitude sickness was cruelly mocking me with an ever-tightening of its ominous vice around my head. As a consequence, I can scarcely recall much detail of the final south northerly Feck Knows, who cares, downward slog into Barranco Huts camp. I simply placed a comforting fleecy hat on my poorly aching head and attempted to immerse myself in 'auto pilot' mode, placing one foot in front of the other with tedious repetition.

It had taken just over three hours from the Lava Tower to finally reach camp at around 16:00. Upon arrival, I dropped down onto a rock and enjoyed a very brief few minutes of utter relief at having reached our temporary home. I was completely exhausted. I then relieved myself of boots, rucksack, poles and full bladder. Within a few moments, I had collapsed into our tent and was sound asleep.

Not even the arrival of Dougie and Simon an hour later woke me up. It was left for Matt to rouse me at 18:00 for the evening meal. I'd missed out on the afternoon delights of popcorn and weak tea. Did I care? Nope. Had my headache improved? Nope. Had it worsened? Yep. I had a quiet word with Asim who dealt me a couple of aspirin, and then shuffled into the mess tent.

It's fair to say that this had been by far the toughest day so far for not only me but for everyone. As a consequence, the atmosphere in the mess tent was rather subdued. I sat quietly in a puddle of my own thoughts as the meal was served.

I felt cold, shivery, nauseous and certainly not hungry in the slightest. Andy was the same. Dougie and Simon, who had both taken an alternative shorter, less rigorous but still established path which avoided the Lava Tower, remained in their tents and had been given *Diamox*; medication to help counteract attitude sickness.

Everyone else seemed ok, albeit tired, and happily tucked into the spread before them. I ate nothing at all. I seriously contemplated returning to my tent for some sulky solitude.

At the end of the meal, 'Milo Mike' very kindly passed me his eponymous drink. It was a caring gesture to raise my spirits off the floor and, to be fair, they reached toenail-high after a few sips - still a very long way from becoming a 'future champion' though.

Assistant guide, Hans, took us through the details of the following day's itinerary and thankfully it would, *mostly*, be reasonably straightforward - combining a distance of only 5¼km (3¼ miles) and an overall gain in altitude of just 48 metres (158 feet). The perfect opportunity to perfect my 'Pole, Pole' skills, obviously without poles.

I say "mostly" straightforward. Within two or three minutes of leaving camp, the route initially takes an almost vertical climb up the 'Barranco Wall'. This 'wall' is a rockface, approximately 250 metres (825 feet) in height, with a weaving rugged path that requires some scrambling in parts to negotiate. This was going to present an early morning physical challenge. And, for anyone without a head for heights, a rather daunting one too.

All I wanted, though, was some rest and, preferably sleep, deep, deep, deep rejuvenating sleep - please! So, I made my excuses and curled up in the comfort of our tent.

In my aching and deluded mind, I offered myself a trade-off of either a gourmet evening in with Nigella Lawson seductively slurping molten dark chocolate off my 'working' pole or simply waking up without a throbber.

Without any prior warning fart whatsoever, nor a niggly tummy, I started to feel a slightly uncomfortable gurgling in my bowel region. Great, that's all I needed! With thoughts of Nigella now on hold, I reluctantly went through the familiar tiresome procedure of putting on a few fleeces, trousers, socks and boots before trudging off to our toilet tent.

Bugger! Perched on my plastic seat it was soon all too obvious that I wasn't releasing any firm stools. I had no choice other than to 'let it go'. I sat there until I was confident I'd emptied myself out then re-trudged my footsteps back to the tent to rummage for some *Imodium* - medication which can usually arrest diarrhoea. To cap it all, I now had to face up to the reality that I had effectively failed my pre-match fitness test for the forthcoming farting competition that night. Far too risky.

Sleep became virtually impossible. First of all, a storm began to brew with heavy rain and a strong wind pummelling our tents.

And then, Dougie went into a manic meltdown. After much coughing and grunting and spitting, and unzipping and zipping, and heavily laboured breathing, he crawled out of his tent, muttered numerous expletives punctuated by grumbled groaning before finally puking-up vociferously.

He went through this wretched routine three times at which point he had, presumably, completely emptied his stomach of any remaining bile and his body of one or two vital organs. He must have felt truly awful. I really did feel very sorry for him but also relieved it wasn't me. I almost, I stress almost, felt inclined to enter his tent and give him a huge cuddle... and juggle with his moobs. That's altitude for you!

All this time the weather was deteriorating badly. The rain was now lashing down, its stair rods attempting to puncture our tents. The howling wind was ferociously snatching at anything not properly secured.

At 03:10, there was an almighty crash. Unbelievably, our toilet tent and 'contents' had been completely uprooted and blown some sixty feet across the camp and into a group of Australians! Not a great time for the Aussies as they'd already lost The Ashes earlier in the year and were now being literally shat on by a group of Poms.

The porters all rushed around frantically trying to repair the mayhem. With shouted laconic instructions and admirable teamwork, I heard, what I presumed to be, our team toilet tent being re-positioned and hammered securely into the rocky ground.

It must have been a good hour before relative calm was restored and the very worst of the storm largely subsided. Our support team had been absolutely incredible in their efforts. I felt so thankful for simply being able to lie nursing my own discomfort in the relative safety of our tent whilst the destruction had unfolded. What a night!

My TOE index took a bit of a hammering too. I'd really struggled today. I felt sick, had a bad headache, had barely eaten, was on the verge of uncontrollable diarrhoea, hadn't been able to fully appreciate the scenery, was tired, couldn't sleep, and had fallen out with my walking poles. I gave it 12 out of 10 (at least it had beaten Spinal Tap's infamous 11).

Chapter 9 – Day 5. Man down

By the time weak tea and 'wash wash' arrived the storm had completely abated, the sky was mostly clear of any clouds and other than the customary farting there was hardly any wind to speak of.

The appalling weather had clearly prevented a frost from forming overnight. Nonetheless the temperature was still not too far off zero. I hadn't recalled any snoring from Dougie and therefore presumed he'd not had any quality sleep at all.

And - no, Nigella wasn't lying next to me with a contented chocolatey smile – but my headache had cleared! In my earlier trade-off thoughts, I had in fact turned 'Gells' down in favour of a clear head. She was probably devastated, and understandably so. As for me... apart from an uncomfortable ache in my stomach, I couldn't have been happier. What an immense relief to be headache-free!

My morale was at an all-time high but was tempered at breakfast following the announcement that Dougie needed to leave the mountain. Asim had made the decision and that was the end of matter.

Also, Steve still looked dreadful but worst of all, the fried eggs were all served without the yolks! Just what was going on?

I absolutely love fried eggs for breakfast and will, first of all, eat all the white leaving one final mouthful of yellow, soft eggy ecstasy on top of an equal-sized piece of toast. Forget Dougie and Steve, the missing yolk was really disappointing. I immediately revoked chef's mountain Michelin stars.

To be blunt, Dougie looked equally as rough as he had appeared following only an hour's trekking on the first day. I guess that was his natural disposition. But, this morning, he had none of his usual 'chirpiness in the face of adversity' about him and he was now also in possession of a persistently hacking cough.

It was a sad farewell as the group hugged Dougie one-by-one and wished him well. Displaying genuine sentiment, he hoped we would all make it to the top.

With Dougie out of earshot, I'm sure I witnessed the most triumphant, yet restrained, fist-clench ever in the history of celebrating through the medium of fist-pumping from his tent-mate, Steve. He was clearly, already thinking about those snore-free nights that now lay ahead as he handed back the earplugs to Matt.

I had nothing but admiration for Dougie and couldn't begin to comprehend how he'd even lasted this long. He'd trekked for ridiculously long hours while suffering from terrible sickness and diarrhoea throughout. His only mistake, a crucial one though, was to underestimate this challenge. He had failed to get adequately fit. This trip, whilst achievable to most people and, arguably, looking 'not too bad' on video clips, demands the greatest respect.

We later learned, after what must have been a Herculean effort, that it had taken Dougie, Mekeke and a porter, ten hours of continuous descent before reaching the safety of a 4x4. Challenging enough even when fully fit I presumed!

Blimey, now I was the elder statesman of our group.

Given that Dougie had been ordered down, I think we all surreptitiously thought that Steve was probably the next obvious candidate for leaving the mountain. Asim must have seen something, though, that had permitted his continued participation. Maybe the *Diamox* was taking some effect but, judging by Steve's general demeanour, it must have been a close call. A monk engrossed in a vow of silence would have had more conversation than Steve, who now was largely hunched over, arms folded, with few signs of emotion in his gaunt face. Perhaps it was simply a case of him too being mightily annoyed at the earlier 'Yolkgate' episode? It was certainly still wrangling with me. But, as the group 'elder' I needed to set an example and reluctantly kept quiet.

Barranco is an interesting camp, pressed up against Kibo, with an open vista opposite an almost vertical, eight hundred and twenty-five feet high rockface. Staring at it after breakfast, I could just about discern the semblance of a path which zig-zagged its way, diagonally from left to right, up to the top.

Apart from all the worries about altitude sickness and the final summit attempt, it was this particular feature that had been of some worry to me.

For many years in my youth I had worked, in the school holidays, high up on roofs without any concerns whatsoever. Climbing up and down scaffolding, carrying tiles and roofing batten and laying them had not bothered me in the slightest. But that had begun to change over the past few years. Being in situations with a sheer drop was beginning to cause me varying degrees of alarm: wobbly legs, anxiety, and the need for verbal 'coaching' from sympathetic, helpful fellow group hikers to help me negotiate particularly tricky terrain being notable symptoms.

So, after self-diagnosing mild acrophobia, I had raised apprehensions about the 'Barranco Wall' or 'Breakfast Wall' as it is sometimes referred to on account of it being tackled very soon after breakfast; usually with egg yolks, I would have thought. Will you just pipe down!

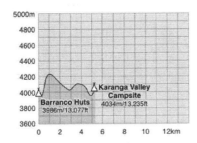

Barranco Huts – Karanga Valley

With Dougie setting off in one direction, the rest of the group headed off over a stream then immediately began the steep ascent. There is no 'easier' alternative route on this section. Therefore, Steve had no option other than to follow, at the rear, very slowly, Asim carrying his rucksack.

Making absolutely certain never ever to look below my own eye level, other than to place my feet or grab a hand-hold on some rock, it was

142

actually quite refreshing to physically climb and occasionally stretch limbs to their limits rather than the usual 'Pole, Pole', plod, plod. Using the recognised terminology, this was a classic 'scramble' in parts, involving a huge variety of hand, arm, foot, leg and knobbly knee movements. A welcome departure from the trudging.

The exertion required for the more extreme scrambling sections, certainly gave our lungs a major workout. Heavy panting and deep breathing being essential in order to feed our bodies of the required oxygen. This led to a concertina effect on occasions, with the group bunching up and grinding to a halt. However, with the exception of Karen requiring one hefty shove from behind and myself needing to be pulled up by grabbing Mike's hand a couple of times, we all proceeded slowly and steadily up the jagged incline without too much trouble.

After forty-five minutes or so, some of our porters had already begun to pass us on the way up which, thankfully, allowed us to pause at regular intervals to give way to them. It was a wonderful opportunity not only to regain my breath but also to press and squeeze myself, with the utmost limpet-like force, back against the rock and finally appreciate the magnificent view, albeit on slightly wobbly legs. Such was my fear of falling forwards, it's possible there's a permanent fossilised impression of my whole body somewhere on that 'wall'.

From these lofty impromptu stopping points, it was exhilarating looking down on Barranco Huts camp far below. The green ranger's office was the most obvious feature, with groups of green and orange tents dotted around it like tiny bugs.

It was quite apparent just how barren the camp and surrounding terrain was. A predominantly hard grey black stony surface with rocks scattered randomly across it. This landscape was occasionally interrupted by narrow, lighter-shaded ground where the well-worn recognised paths flowed. Tree groundsels and dark green scrub with fleeting hints of yellow were the only discernible vegetation. This repeating pattern of rock and scrub seemed to stretch downwards for miles upon miles before finally merging with the brown plains of lowland Tanzania.

Throughout the trip, we had all frequently referred to and been astonished by the super-human feats of the porters. And now, here they were almost effortlessly lugging all the equipment up this extremely steep rocky incline. Absolutely amazing! Perhaps they'd had the egg yolks? Yep, I was still annoyed.

After an hour and a half, and with an enormous sense of achievement and no small amount of relief, I became the eighth member of our team to reach the top of the Barranco Wall. I couldn't see Steve but assumed he was very cautiously creeping up at a pace that suited him. I didn't think he'd been forced to turn back but the thought had crossed my mind?

Once clear of the vertical section of the 'wall', there was a short, level stroll across some enormous flat slabs of rock to a viewing point which, arguably, rivalled any viewing platform anywhere. I say 'arguably', for we were now high above an impenetrable cloud base that obscured the vast wild Tanzanian plains below but I'm sure the view *was* breathtaking, I just couldn't see it. It was reminiscent of peering out of an airplane window above the clouds only, here, this was strictly al fresco with an Executive Business Class volume of legroom.

However, behind us seemingly much closer now, and in stark clear view, was the overwhelming presence of Kibo acting as a canvas of dark volcanic rock upon which was haphazardly drawn a dazzling patchwork of snow, ice, icicles and the precariously sloping Heim Glacier. The water-induced artistry glistened like intricately embroidered sequins on an ivory-coloured veil in the white, hot African sunshine. An unblemished cyan sky provided the perfect backdrop for this magnificent geological creation.

Things would only go downhill from here but only because, at just shy of 14,000 feet, we were already at today's highest point.

The mood was very jovial and optimistic now as we progressed across a rocky desert landscape with a predominantly gentle downwards gradient. It was relatively easy-going. I was able to not only keep up with the other members of the group but also chat and walk at the same time. How cool! And, if that wasn't cool enough, I was now wearing my cool sports shades and had fashioned a bandana out of my multi-purpose paisley-print buff which, according to the packaging, could be worn in at least a dozen different 'cool' styles, none of which I would have attempted in public without hours of diligent 'cool' practice in front of a mirror. If only those blonde twins could have seen the 'cool' me now; would they have been able to resist striking up a conversation with me? Would I have needed to have fended them off with my pole? Is there any need to answer either of those questions?

On Kilimanjaro, there are occasional route signs. Like the ones used for public footpaths in the UK, these are usually a single wooden stake upon which is a perpendicularly placed flatter piece of wood pointing in the direction of the route(s). The lettering is consistently yellow and 4 or 5 inches in height, perfectly matching the signage at the very top of the mountain which I'd longingly stared at many times online during my research.

Such a sign caught my eye. It stated: "This Trail is Prohibited". I wondered why? My inner Pandora was bursting with curiosity. Back home, I have to confess that I always translate such signs as meaning: "Wow, this could be of great interest and possibly includes an element of danger" and then proceed with huge excitement, usually negotiating walls, fences and a generous quantity of barbed wire.

It's seldom that I strike gold and find something of genuine interest but I do usually rip my trousers. I most certainly do not condone such behaviour though! Looking up, beyond the sign, was an array of sheer rock faces, ice and glaciers, huge boulders, and evidence of landslides. It was patently clear to me that the whole landscape did not only provide an element of danger but the whole periodic table. So, I happily followed the group along the designated trail.

Our mid-morning stop witnessed much frivolity amongst the group and soon the remainder of our support team appeared in the form of a smiling, singing line of porters making ridiculously light work of all the bags and kit on their backs, shoulders and heads. We were also joined by a few expectant, aptly named, white-necked ravens, presumably hoping for some snacks. These birds were almost identical to the all-black ravens back home. A spot-the-difference competition would have been concluded in an instant.

As with each day on this trip, we were continually reacquainted with our porters who were either overtaking us or having a well-earned rest. The same old, perpetually cheery faces would broadly grin up at us day after day.

I recognised one such porter, sporting a Bob Marley t-shirt and, such was my buoyant disposition, gave him the customary down-with-the-kids greeting of knuckles banging together, followed by a gladiatorial handshake, finished off with a sort of thumb-wrestle. Trust me, it's so cool when performed effortlessly by an African but uncomfortably awkward when attempted by this Englishman abroad.

Thankfully, he appreciated my gesture with a heart-warming smile. And, of course, I should have left it at that but, oh no, I had to go one step further. Such was my confidence and elation that I broke out into a simple and possibly tuneful "One love..." (the classic Bob Marley song) in deference to his t-shirt, to which 'Bob' immediately accompanied me obviously anticipating a spontaneous duet.

I should have guessed that he would know the entire song word-perfectly whereas I could only recall the lyrics "One love" and something about 'getting together' and 'feeling alright'. So, I pretended to have a tickly cough and shuffled off in my awkward-Englishman-abroad sort of way and fumbled in my rucksack for a shovel with which to dig myself a hole. I guess it was a high-altitude version of Dads' dancing at weddings. At least my kids weren't there to cringe with embarrassment, nor was I wearing socks with sandals.

But my spirits were so high that I simply couldn't leave it on a (Bob Marley) low note. So, by saying "Jambo" (Swahili for hello) I struck up a conversation with another porter. I'd recognised him from the previous days as the one who usually only had one single facial expression – that of smiling – and when not smiling he was either laughing or singing.

And, with a cheeky grin he introduced himself as "David Cameron". We enjoyed a most light-hearted conversation. Apparently, he had previously gone by the name of Tony Blair. Writing this now, I wonder if he is now known as Theresa.

The trail remained fairly easy until there was a sharp descent of five hundred feet into a picturesque valley where there was a glistening, babbling stream. This is the final place to collect water before the summit and would have been a delightful place to stop and have a snack were it not for the fact that our next camp was now only half an hour away. So, we pressed on up a steep, switch-back path and soon arrived at Karanga Camp.

If first impressions were important then no one had informed this camp. It was bleak, barren, on a slope and, even at only 13:00, felt damp and cool in the bright sunshine.

After lunch, we embarked upon our routine acclimatisation hike and headed further up the mountain across the bleak and barren landscape; this whole area was in fact consistently bleak and barren. Why not go the whole hog and rename this place Bleak & Barren Camp (upon returning home I decided to look up the meaning of Karanga. It appears to be Swahili for 'peanut/groundnut'. In Maori it is a ceremonial call of welcome to visitors. Not one single mention of 'bleak and barren').

You may have gathered that I hadn't exactly warmed to this chilly camp. Not only that but, at 4,034 metres (13,235 feet), it was only marginally higher than when we'd set off from Barranco Huts after breakfast, and still way below the highest I'd ever been before on foot; 4,627 metres (15,180 feet) at the Lava Tower. And, if that wasn't enough, I'd developed another headache.

Back in camp it was pleasing to see that Steve had arrived safely but it was quite obvious that he wouldn't have required any make-up or acting skills to become an extra in *Dawn of the Zombie Mountain Menace II*. The last time I'd seen such a pale face was on an anaemic snowman and Steve appeared to have only sufficient energy to carry the weight of his own clothes.

I decided not to tell him to 'man-up' but instead welcomed him to this lovely camp. I didn't have the heart to mention its 'bleak and barrenness'; I think that would have finished him off. He slunk off to his tent. I trudged off to join Matt in our tent.

We now had plenty of time to rest and, because we'd seen sufficient bleak and barren landscape, we whiled the time away with frivolous chatter and went through the usual process of unpacking and packing followed by yet more unpacking and packing.

Suddenly, Matt surprisingly produced an aerosol can of DEET from his rucksack. In silence, he held it aloft with an air of incredulity. I stared back in astonishment, quickly realising that this, despite my headache, was banter manna from Heaven.

On this adventure, one key attribute of the intrepid trekker is to have the ability to manage the weight and contents of one's day pack in accordance with predicted requirements for that day's hike; maybe only a maximum of six or seven hours.

Poor Matt might just as well have placed a 'yes, I know - schoolboy error' yellow sticky on his forehead and texted me an invitation to adopt 'piss-take mode' - which I did. Even *I* knew, and I certainly made sure Matt was aware too, that mosquitos aren't found at these altitudes. In fact, he'd unnecessarily carried the DEET to approximately a staggering eight-and-a-half thousand feet (almost equivalent of two Ben Nevi, or should that be 'Neves'? Altitude once again playing havoc with thought processes) *above* the known mosquito zone. The cannister, arguably, warranted an entry in the *Guinness Book of Records*.

148

Needless to say, suitably embarrassed, he transferred the wholly redundant stowaway into his kit bag and, in trying to change the topic of conversation, reminded me of 'he-weegate'. For the record, it was actually: 'Teepee, 'tea pee' Tentgate' but who was I to correct him.

The hilarity inevitably led to farting but upon releasing my first worthy effort, I sensed something was amiss. Upon rapid, concerned inspection I discovered it was indeed the dreaded 'D-word' - and not Dougie. It wasn't so much a skid mark, more a delicate pool rather similar to a melted chocolate button.

Over the past few days of trial and error, I'd eventually compiled a must-have mental list of all mandatory requirements for a successful visit to the toilet. So, following yet more unpacking and packing of stuff sacks, I quickly gathered together the: wet wipes, antibacterial hand gel, headtorch, a fresh pair of pants, and a carrier bag in which to ferry back my soiled ones. What else could I have needed?

I didn't feel able to use our group toilet tent. I thought it unfair to the other members of the team as well as to the porter who would have to deal with 'it'. So, I laboured in the rapidly cooling air to find a wooden 'long-drop' camp version.

Upon entering the fetid structure, I switched on my headtorch, turned the corner and was confronted with an appalling, gut-wrenching sight of human excrement plastered all over the wooden floor and some creeping up the sides of this abominable diabolical excuse of a toilet. It was like a herd of incontinent cows had been the previous visitors. Not that farmyard manure particularly disturbs me but there is something innately repulsive about the human variety, especially when sitting in amongst it might be required. This was stomach-churningly vile! The only redeeming feature of this ghastly place was that all the germs and bacteria had moved out in disgust; a bog bug boycott.

I retreated as quickly as was slowly possible at this altitude and found an alternative venue not too far away. In complete contrast, and to much relief, this was one was comparatively clean and dry albeit bloody cold. I spotted only one solitary jobbie lurking behind the hole in the floor. In a brilliant moment of Karanga Camp choreography, I carefully positioned my feet either side of it, placed my toiletry bag within arm's reach, rolled down my trousers and pants and made sure they were secured above the floor by widening my stance slightly, pulled up my down jacket to well above my bottom area and held it in position with my chin, and then, in this contorted squatting position, finally released my bowels.

At the best of times the evacuation of diarrhoea is a fairly unpleasant experience but standing in a position which could only have otherwise been contrived during a game of *Twister* at in excess of 13,000 feet and with a lurking turd waiting for just one careless lapse meant my shaking thighs and screaming leg muscles simply couldn't cope for a moment longer. I clenched my rasping bottom sphincter and stood up for some urgently needed relief. Here I was, stood in a dark, desperately pathetic toilet, with my mouth now beginning to experience that slight salivation process before being sick, shivering with cold, trying to avoid standing in excrement, and with small trickles of diarrhoea running down the insides of my legs; at least *that* was a warm sensation.

I have to admit, in my dystopian despair, I experienced a deeply personal wobbly moment when I could have whimpered ever so slightly. But, as is the arguably outdated English way, crying wasn't an option so I paused for reflection and indulged in an honest, forthright heart-to-heart chat with myself: "This is fucking rubbish! This is a fucking shit hole. Wouldn't be at all surprised if some cunt of a cleaner comes barging in to give this 'crap trap' its long overdue decontamination. Well it was your idea to come. You knew there'd be moments like this. Come on, let's get this over with, re-join Matt and just move on…"

So, I tried to deal, as well as possible, with my current pitiful predicament. Not many options presented themselves to me. The resigned conclusion was to regain my awkward squatting position, stop feeling sorry for myself and get on with the job in hand and it has to be noted, rather repulsively, partly *on* my hand.

In my lonely haunt I must have repeated this squatting and standing up procedure four or five times and only when being absolutely sure that I'd emptied myself did I begin the arduous task of meticulously cleaning up. Thank goodness for wet wipes. I'd had enough by now and couldn't be arsed to change my pants. I'd simply have to 'wear' the chocolate button back to camp and deal with it inside the tent. However, I'd successfully negotiated a deeply morale-sapping experience and took comfort in the fact that it couldn't really get any worse... I stepped outside and then puked up. Thank goodness for wet wipes, again. I just wish I'd brought some water with me though! If I'd have been offered an immediate evacuation and transportation home, I'd have been seriously tempted. Surely this was as low as things could fucking get!

After reaching camp again - ok, it was only fifty yards away and all downhill but it felt like a genuine trek in its own right - I requested two aspirin from Asim who first gave me a comprehensive consultation about my headache and then handed over two tablets. Thankfully, I'd passed his examination.

Back in our tent, I advised Matt that he should look away. Following much puffing and panting, I successfully changed my pants and placed the 'chocolately' ones in the carrier bag and sealed it with the tightest knot possible.

Next, I unpacked everything yet again in order to find the *Imodium*. When administering medication it's always important to read the instructions on the packet. So, I popped a handful of tablets, reached for my reading glasses, which I recalled had appeared during the unpacking process, and then learned that two *Imodium* tablets should be taken initially followed by, if required, one tablet after every loose bowel movement, and no more than four tablets should be taken per day, for a maximum of two days. And finally, if the diarrhoea persists for more than forty-eight hours then contact should be made with a doctor. All very good advice of course but there wasn't a section on

151

what to do at thirteen thousand feet without a mobile signal. At this point I would have failed a drugs test.

I then sulked in my sleeping bag, waiting for the drugs to work, reliving the toilet episode in my mind and still feeling resentment over the egg yolks.

Surprisingly and thankfully, by the time of our evening meal my state of health had bottomed-out and I was beginning to feel ever so slightly better; the medication was taking effect and I'd drunk two litres of water containing hydration salts. This delicately grapefruit-flavoured water was actually a hugely welcome change after days of drinking the boiled and sterilised variety. Poor old Steve, though, was confined to his tent.

Our group was in high spirits not least because it was Olivia's fortieth and Karen had brought all Olivia's birthday cards with her. Naturally, we all sang 'Happy Birthday' and wished her well, then the chef entered the mess tent carrying a freshly-made birthday cake! Wow! Unbelievable!

Once again, we all bowed down to his high-altitude culinary skills. And then, that shilling dropped again... he'd undoubtedly used the egg yolks to produce this gastronomic masterpiece. If we'd have been on the *Great British Bake Off,* Mary Berry would, I'm sure, have described it as a 'show stopper' and our chef would undoubtedly have been named 'Baker of the Week'.

In our opinion, he'd have won the whole show. I felt a tiny bit of guilt about my earlier disappointment at not having had eggs yolks at breakfast. It was a good job I hadn't continually stewed over it in my thoughts all day.

The brief for the following day all sounded rather straightforward and fairly easy. We would depart at 08:00 and head towards the final camp on the ascent route, namely Barafu Huts. It was not a particularly long distance, at only 3½km (just a mosquito's todger over 2 miles, not that there are any mozzies at this altitude, right, Matt?) but it was a fairly relentless uphill climb, quite steep in parts, of 628 metres (2,060 feet).

Then, at 23:00 we would have to 'get up' and be ready for breakfast ahead of the summit attempt. Effectively, the following day's hike to the next camp *and* the beginning of the summit attempt would both take place on the same day.

Lying in my sleeping bag, I reflected on what had been a roller-coaster of a day; literal highs and lows as well as physical and emotional ones. In fact, Nigella could once again have come knocking (or unzipping) with her tiresome offers but all I wanted was to wake up in the morning feeling as fully fit as possible. The route today hadn't been too strenuous but I didn't like the camp, one toilet would have been on the World Health Organization's 'to be condemned' list and I'd hit a desperately low mental moment!

Conversely, though, I was beginning to feel better. Consequently, my TOE index was 11 out 10. Referring back to the previous day's TOE, I noted that things had improved, so it wasn't all bad.

Chapter 10 – Day 6. Easy going

I can't claim to have enjoyed much sleep that night but I had rested well. I certainly hadn't missed Dougie's snoring. My mind simply wouldn't stop processing the previous day's events as well as excitedly looking forward. Additionally, I felt a slight reluctance to fall into a deep sleep in case of a further chocolate button incident and I had no idea where my spare pants were; if indeed I'd packed any others?

However, Matt was extremely really very eager to report that I'd 'experienced' apnoea during the night. My first reaction was to check my pants. And then I remembered. Yes, he too, had indulged in much pre-trip research and his favourite snippet was the subject of apnoea. It's a condition when the body actually stops breathing for a period of, usually, ten to fifteen seconds before continuing as normal. It's not uncommon at high altitudes but is, if unaware, quite alarming for the tent-mate. I'd been completely oblivious but Matt had been fascinated when, at one stage, I took my 'final breath' eventually followed some ten seconds later by another one.

I considered that he might have made this story up just so he could spout high and mightily from his recently acquired mountain medical repertoire. Maybe it was a ploy to make me forget DEETgate? (too late, I'd already recorded it in my travel diary and it's now in this book.) But, the genuine delighted enthusiasm with which he described the event convinced me that I had indeed had a bout of apnoea; definitely something to brag about down the pub. It was just a pity it didn't produce a gruesome lengthy scar. It's always far more impressive when a rolled trouser leg, or similar, can reveal a partly healed wound.

Weak tea and 'wash wash' as usual signalled the start of a new day and it was bloody freezing; maybe 5 degrees below zero. The bleak and barren landscape of Karanga had remained bleak and barren but, during the night, had frosted over in a sly, cunning attempt to seem more appealing. Yep, all white, icy, crystalline and sparkling in the morning sun. The full frosty gamut in fact. Well, let me tell you, it didn't fool me.

The warm clothes at the bottom of my sleeping bag were, as usual, an uplifting treat. However, it was so cold, that the solution my contact lenses were in felt only marginally above freezing and upon insertion, my lenses produced a reflex response in the form of a stream of tears. Thankfully, a few blinks cleared everything and I made a note to place my box of lenses at the bottom of my sleeping bag in future. It would be getting quite crowded down there at night.

Then I applied the equally icy cold roll-on deodorant to my cowering armpits. That too, would now be added to the 'bottom of the bag at night time' list - 'Gells' would have to go.

Finally, I stared hesitantly at what might just as well have been a bag of frozen peas... nope, I just couldn't face a freshen-up with the nearly-frozen wet wipes yep, tick, added to the 'bottom of the bag' list - so I let that particular act of personal hygiene slip on this occasion. I felt as though I'd just been admitted to the proper really rugged explorers club. No doubt, I smelled like it too.

Once again, Asim was the bringer of bad news: Simon would be leaving us! Apparently, he'd endured a very rough night, even by his previous appalling standards. His headache was extreme and he had also now developed a very concerning cough. It wasn't a 'normal' cough and was of sufficient concern to Asim for him to be immediately led down off the mountain to safety.

Was it severe AMS we probably all wondered but didn't like to ask. Perhaps his condition was verging on either of HACO (High Altitude Cerebral Oedema) or HAPO (High Altitude Pulmonary Oedema)?

So, without joining us for breakfast, Simon departed with an assistant guide. It was a brief farewell. He appeared almost too delicate to hug but we all did, very gently. Only a few heart-felt words were exchanged and he was off. It was as deeply sad as it had been all too obviously inevitable.

Like with Dougie, I was surprised that Simon had managed to get as far as he had. Whereas Dougie had been overtly, noisily poorly, by contrast Simon had been distant and mostly silent. Dougie was experienced at hiking but not fit. Simon, who was far younger, was also experienced but also very fit. Both, though, had arrived at the same fate. Trip over!

Talk about a reality check! It was a blunt reminder that Kilimanjaro is not to be taken lightly, does not easily embrace human life and can strike indiscriminately at any time. There are no guarantees whatsoever on this mountain.

And then there were eight. I immediately thought of the Genesis album '...And Then There Were Three...'. Admittedly, the Prog Rock specialists had lost two members of the calibre of Peter Gabriel and Steve Hackett whereas we'd *only* lost Simon and Dougie; no disrespect guys. Genesis would eventually achieve greatness by turning 'mainstream'. By effectively continuing 'upstream' I hoped we would achieve ours. So, at 08:00, it was *Follow You, Follow Me* out of camp. Not since the All Blacks, led by Richie McCaw, had there been a more tightly-knit eight.

I was so relieved to have left Karanga Camp behind. It had certainly lacked atmosphere, in both senses of the word, and, did I mention, I'd found it barren and bleak... or was it bleak and barren? Plus, it was cold, on a slope, included at least one long-drop toilet that wasn't fit for bacterial sewer spawn let alone a human, and had finally finished off poor old Simon. If there had been a Karanga Camp souvenir shop, I would have boycotted it... that is, unless it had sold toilet cleaning kits and those rubber gloves without the cotton flock lining.

We were now well into the realms of dramatic stark scenery. There was scant vegetation but this was more than made up for by the imposing backdrop of Kibo, looming on our left-hand side, adorned with snow, impenetrable ice sheets and glaciers. The very ground we walked upon was more or less exactly as I imagined the lunar surface to be and the volcanic dust provided me with yet another opportunity to publicly display my buff.

It really was a wonderful day to be out and about with barely a breeze in the crisp rarified air and the dazzling sun providing a warming presence in a rich blue sky. By late morning, it was possible to see various buildings and structures of Barafu Camp high up on a distant ridge. They didn't look at all far away but, by now, the pace was markedly 'Pole, Pole' so it was simply a question of pressing on, knowing there was no rush whatsoever.

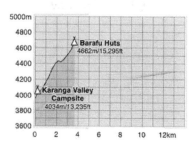

Karanga Valley – Barafu Huts

As I had learned from early on in this trek, I continued to make progress at my own pace making absolutely sure that I never reached the stage of panting or puffing too hard. Matt, as had often been the case, was happy to be with me at the back of the group and we also enjoyed some quality time with the ever-cheerful Asim. His love for this mountain was evident.

The landscape may have been bleak but I felt it had a captivating beauty. Yes, in terms of colour it was a largely one-dimensional volcanic grey but this was abruptly intruded upon by huge glaciers glistening with a diamond-like lustre. The rocky granules crunched beneath our heavy boots sending ribbons of fine dust trails across the alien terrain. The bright, warm sun was generating a mood of optimism and a glowing sense of well-being... and it was oh so wonderfully quiet. In those moments, I felt blissfully far removed from civilisation. I was completely immersed in a harmonious sense of tranquillity and isolation.

I'd read that the 'long-drop' toilets at the next camp had been rebuilt after a lady had fallen to her death when the entire structure had collapsed down the side of the mountain. We were now close enough to see the 'new' toilet block and it certainly appeared to be perched precariously on the edge of a ridge. I was sure our blue team toilet would be safely placed on solid ground nowhere near an edge, cliff or any other potentially worrying precipice.

Soon there was a twenty-five-minute final scramble up a steep slope where we were met by a sign in yellow lettering stating 'Barafu Hut', marking our entrance into camp. We signed in at the ranger's office, protected by the usual green corrugated pitched roof, and then made our way to the tents.

This was our Base Camp. Wow, what an achievement to have reached this far! I'd had no idea what to expect. At first, I was quite surprised by how heavily populated it was with dozens of brightly coloured tents pitched on the firm ground amongst the rocks and many hikers milling, seemingly aimlessly, around. Perhaps they were simply killing time, dissipating nervous energy before the summit attempt.

The ranger's office, toilet block and the odd isolated 'long-drop' appeared to be the only permanent structures, with the whole camp maybe spread out over the area of a football pitch. We were now at 4,662 metres (15,295 feet, or eleven WBs), the highest I'd ever been on foot.

This really did feel very high up but, at 15,180 feet, it also placed some perspective on the comparatively extraordinary height of the Lava Tower that we'd conquered a couple of days ago. I recalled feeling awful at the Lava Tower and wanting to descend as quickly as possible. Here, though, despite a headache and upset tummy, I felt nicely calm and enjoyed an enormous sense of achievement. It was apparent that the acclimatisation process was working to my benefit. A huge relief.

Our tents were positioned at the far end of the camp towards a saddle and valley, the other side of which was the jagged Mawenzi; a dramatic mountain in its own right.

Matt and I fell into our tent, threw our rucksacks and kit bags into the far end, tied back the flaps and simply sat and stared at the most incredible view. I was too much out of breath to speak but even if I could have, I wouldn't have. It was a moment to savour in silence. The silence was only interrupted by a summoning for lunch.

It was then, when we sprang out of our tent and took a couple of paces, that the effects of the high altitude were plainly evident. The lack of oxygen really did stop me abruptly in my tracks and walking thereafter was carried out at an unbelievably slow pace. It was almost comical to witness others walking like this too.

It wasn't at all painful or concerning, rather, it was completely fascinating and compelling to experience my body react in this way. Taking a breath was now an act I was fully conscious of as opposed to something that 'ran' in the background. It was quite bizarre and verged on the euphoric. I loved it. Simply by writing about it now, I crave for this sensation again. For me, it was an ecstatically surprising addiction.

I commenced lunch with a starter of two aspirin tablets and a litre of water and then picked at the customary wonderful spread that was laid before us. I didn't really have much of an appetite but wasn't too concerned. My ambivalence may have been due to the effect of the altitude or possibly because I'd already been experiencing a lack of appetite on the trip. It was all perfectly normal and not something to be overly concerned with. A daily calorie deficit over a period of a week is something which, for most people, the body can compensate for by using stored energy in bodily fat.

There was now an option for one final acclimatisation walk out of the camp, up to a height of around 4,800 metres (approximately 15,800 feet) – "wevs", I thought, with infantile altitude-affected dismissal! Perhaps there was much soul-searching and reluctance but we all elected to take advantage of this walk.

Back at camp, I chose to use our beloved blue toilet tent for what disappointingly turned out to be diarrhoea again. It was a bit of a blow, especially as my headache was showing encouraging signs of improvement. But now, after taking yet more *Imodium*, it was simply time to rest.

As the sun began to dip out of view, Matt and I stood outside our tent and watched the mystical swirling silver clouds wafting up through the valley before dissolving into the cooler mountain air. It was a beautiful and transfixing endless cycle unfurling in the deafening silence which filled this craggy arena; another of Mother Earth's little gems that perhaps most of us fail to genuinely appreciate. By the time the sun finally disappeared, the temperature was close to freezing point so we slowly rapidly retreated into the relative warmth of our tent.

At dinner, the atmosphere in the mess tent was unusually subdued. There was a hint of concerned anticipation and the childish joking had evidently been left further down the mountain. Yes, we'd come this far but there remained the small matter of the hardest part yet to come. A team of ten had become eight, we'd reached base camp with all of us - naturally, with the exception of 'Matt the Unaffected' - to varying degrees, suffering from ailments due to the high altitude. Every one of the 'normal' seven had a headache and was not particularly hungry. Steve and myself also had diarrhoea. No one, though, had any blisters or muscle aches and pains. Little wonder, by the time Asim joined us, there was still plenty of food remaining on the table, despite Matt's best efforts to consume everything and anything.

It was now time for the following day's briefing. I say 'the following day' but, as already mentioned, 'tomorrow' was due to commence at 23:00 tonight. This was the big one and so, not surprisingly, it was Head Guide, Asim, who took us through the details.

'Tomorrow' would begin with an unusually early breakfast at 23:00 before heading out of camp and up Kibo, predominantly on a series of switch-backs, before emerging at the crater rim at Stella Point to coincide with the sunrise. Distances were largely an irrelevant statistic but the increase in altitude of 1,083 metres (3,553 feet) certainly wasn't. We would then enjoy a hot drink before the final leg of the gentler upwards journey to Uhuru Peak; *only* an extra 150 metres (493 feet) in altitude.

Following the mandatory photos and short time of appreciation it would be back down to Barafu, a short rest and snack, and then down to Millennium Hut camp for the night. I wasn't particularly interested in any distances or heights for this final section. I had only one thing on my mind – Uhuru Peak.

Asim's voice was so soft and calm, to the point of soothing. Whenever he paused, there was a deadening and thoughtful silence within the confines of the mess tent. The space we were seated in seemed to contract around me with intense intimacy. His hushed, captive audience was hypnotised and mesmerised by every single last word.

Asim had made it sound so very simple. Hmm? It was virtually impossible to comprehend the task ahead as a series of simple consecutive events as outlined by our fatherly head guide; it just felt like one mammoth undertaking looming on the horizon. For me, it was like waiting for the final call before a surgical procedure. All of us, with adrenalin and, in some cases diarrhoea, surging, simply wanted to crack on with the final ascent.

First on our 'to do' list was to plan what to wear for breakfast later that night. Naturally, this process involved the tedious task of unpacking everything, yet again.

In my now, well-documented, pre-climb research I'd started to read all about the trade winds' effect on Kilimanjaro but quickly began to glaze over as it reminded me of some particularly indecipherable and boring Geography lessons at school. In reality, all I was interested in was what temperature might be anticipated on summit night. So, cutting to the chase, I learned to expect somewhere in the region of -20° Celsius on a still night, and if unlucky enough to have to factor it in, then, with an element of wind chill it might feel a tad chillier, at -40°. That's all I needed to know – bloody cold, then.

I had tried to recall the lowest temperature I'd ever been in outdoors and came to the conclusion it was probably in the region of -a little bit°. But that was all fine, that's what research is for and I'd packed accordingly. It also meant that no one could quote that annoying phrase which pompous grey-haired, bearded GORE-TEX® 4x4 Ramblers (and that's just the women) often self-righteously spout out in the south of England: "There is no such thing as bad weather, only the wrong clothes". Well, I can assure these people that 'bad weather' had been alive and kicking arse at Barranco Camp. Anyone foolhardy enough to have been 'outdoors' that night would have had *any* clothing ripped off them in seconds.

Back home, I had diligently compiled a reasonable list of what to take with me and had soon discovered I possessed virtually none of it. So, I bought a store discount card at a well-known excellent, specialist retailer with 'Outdoors' and 'Go' in their name and, arguably, became their No.1 customer for a couple of months. Not that I received any official recognition; even a 40g blueberry energy bar and a photo in their staff magazine would have been nice.

On one particular visit, I entered the store armed with my 'summit night' list. Because the key to staying warm is 'layering' my intention was to build up my clothing from a base layer right up to an outer jacket. So, my basket was eventually filled with a thermal base layer, a technical t-shirt, one fleece size small, one fleece size medium, one fleece size large, one gilet, one fleece size x-large, one x-large down jacket, and one x-large jacket that was both windproof and waterproof.

Obviously, I needed to try all the items on, and in size order, to make sure my Russian Doll system would work. The fitting rooms' sign clearly stated that no more than 3 items could be taken in; I had 9! I explained the situation to a most helpful sales assistant who fully understood my intentions. She handed me one of those fitting rooms' tags bearing a number '3' on it. This was very quickly followed by the handing over of two more identical tags, to make the 9. We both giggled. I, plus two baskets overflowing with clothing and three tags, was then permitted to proceed.

Eventually, and by only just managing to swivel my now biscuit barrel-like body around inside the once spacious confines of the cubicle, I admired myself in the mirror... hmm..., not bad. It was worthy of an appreciative eyebrow-raise. Amazingly it had all come together rather well, each layer had neatly fitted on top of the one below.

Mind you, I hadn't sweated so much since I'd been accidentally locked in a Swedish sauna with my good friend Nigel and some charming, overly friendly ladies: Helga, Astrid, Tuva and Greta. It was following the Euro 1992 final in Gothenburg. We'd all been to the match. The ladies were Danish, Denmark had just been crowned the football champions of Europe and they mentioned something about '*probably* the best pork in the world.' An easy mistake. We nearly brought the bacon home though. Enough of that though; what goes on in a sauna stays in the sauna.

Inside our cosy tent, now doubling up as a Men's fitting room, Matt and I compared our respective wardrobes for our breakfast date later that evening, most keen to avoid the potential embarrassment of wearing exactly the same attire. Well, we're both modern men. Our clothing didn't clash but Matt clearly felt the cold less than me; he *only* had six layers.

Furthermore, I had a pair of inner gloves and really warm outer mittens, a fleecy hat, a pair of thermal long johns, hiking trousers (obviously with the lower leg sections zipped on), and an outer pair of windproof and waterproof leggings. My faithful and highly comfortable Salomon boots would be worn over an inner pair of cotton socks on top of which would be a delightfully fluffy woolly thermal pair.

With the exception of my outer water and windproof jacket, I planned to start the summit attempt wearing everything. I felt there was enough to contend with without having the added burden and concern of feeling cold right from the outset.

Knowing the importance of drinking water, we both chose to carry two litres in our Camelbak bladders plus one litre in an aluminium flask. And finally, we packed three snack bars each. I say finally, but I also had a special treat; something I'd read about in my research.

This was the lightest my rucksack had been all week.

So, that was it, we were fully prepared. Now what? Well, it was impossible to pace up and down so I opened up Henry's guidebook and started to read out loud his description of summit night. It was quite tricky reading fluently at this altitude, and I was pausing for breath at the end of every sentence, but it was a clammy-hand-inducing reminder of what lay ahead.

And, while the exact details may have drifted in and out of our consciousness, certain phrases such as "...chilling your bones and numbing the marrow...", "...but it's a painful, tear-inducing half-hour on sheer scree..." certainly hit the target and stuck fast. It was rather similar to watching *Dr Who* as a child. Yes, it was certainly terrifyingly scary but virtually impossible to look away as a Cyberman appeared from nowhere. Compelling horror. Following my impromptu '*Jackanory* at Altitude Special', together with questions from the enthralled audience (Matt), we were only half an hour closer to breakfast.

Batteries? Well done Matt! We eagerly searched for spare headtorch and camera batteries to pack in the safety of a warm inside pocket. We were now three minutes closer to breakfast.

Farting, due to my bowel situation, was currently not on the agenda and I-spy only produced, "something beginning with FM?" - "Fucking Mess"; referring to the inside of our tent. I think Matt was attempting to make a point. But, a small 'domestic' wasn't going to break our bond and we happily progressed to variations: "ARFM"? - "A Right...", "LATRFMIH"? - "Look at the right FM in here". All hilarious of course. We were now a useful fifteen minutes closer to breakfast.

Next on the agenda was an intellectual medical debate on whether or not to take *Diamox*. We didn't reach a conclusion but another ten minutes elapsed.

In the very highly unlikely event of both of us falling asleep, we discussed whether it was worth setting an alarm. The answer we unanimously arrived at, by two votes to none, was yes. The reasoning, however, was not to ensure we would be woken up on time but because neither of us had a clue how to set an alarm on a mobile phone and therefore it might keep us occupied for a good hour or so. Oh, how we laughed.

Next, Matt rummaged in his rucksack and pulled out an envelope which appeared to be the sort that would contain a greetings card. He explained that he'd been wondering when to give it to me and then handed it across the bags and general mess that untidily separated us; but which, would not break us. What on Earth was it? I tentatively ripped it open and pulled out a card.

The front said 'Good Luck' and upon opening it up there was a series of good luck messages from the Year 3 children at school; the ones I'd given the presentation on mountains to. I'd already been presented with a good luck card from Mrs Binout and my two children prior to leaving for Heathrow (which, being superstitious, I'd been carrying in my rucksack all week and had read every night) as well as a few witty and generally unhelpful texts from friends but certainly hadn't expected anything else. It was extremely heart-warming to read all their brief but hugely encouraging words. It certainly made me smile. And then, one message brought a tear to my eyes: "Good luck Mister Mountain Man. I hope you get to the top. Danny". *He* was wishing *me* good luck in my relatively inconsequential challenge whilst he was facing a far bigger battle which I don't think he fully comprehended or, rather, he viewed it all so differently to an adult. I read his words a few times. So simple, so unselfish, so innocent.

My beautiful darling daughter had lovingly given me a good luck 'charm' to take with me. I checked my zipped trouser pocket for it. It was safely tucked away. A huge comfort! It's such a deeply personal and precious 'charm' that I have had it on my person EVERY day since!

As the evening wore on, we both began to feel the need to simply rest in the silence of our own thoughts and were only interrupted by the call of nature and all the associated faffing around that arose as a consequence. It was still a most compelling novelty being rendered breathless by even the simplest of tasks.

It's at idle times, such as enjoying a bottle of wine outside on the patio on a summer's evening, or simply trying to get back to sleep, when my mind goes into a frenzy of random, unconnected thoughts. I have no control over it whatsoever. It's a feral part of my being that I simply have to accept. Sometimes I enjoy the ride, sometimes not. Tonight, in a cosy tent at nearly 5,000 metres in altitude, was certainly conducive to such imaginative activity.

I thought of my immediate family back at home. My two children would be asleep, of that I was sure. My wife, however, probably not, knowing that soon I'd be setting off for the final 'push'. Mrs Binout had been truly amazing: she'd accepted and tolerated my incessant, selfish training programme for five months. And now, for the past week or so, she'd had to deal with two young children — school runs, homework, meals etc – as well as a stressful job. The people behind the people are often the real heroes.

And then philosophical meanderings began to intrude upon my thoughts. The 1963 film, *Jason and the Argonauts*, had made a huge impression on me as a child. As part of the plot, the Gods on Mount Olympus were, at times, 'playing' with the destiny of Jason on his quest for the Golden Fleece - honestly, if it was a fleece he was after then he only needed to look in my kit bag. I wondered whether the outcome of my quest was already predetermined? Perhaps I could change my destiny if it wasn't as I'd wished for? Patience! Only time would reveal my fate.

I even pondered the lazy brazen chameleon and sparkly diamond butterfly that I'd seen earlier in the week. I hoped they were both ok.

I'm not sure whether either of us slept at all but we certainly rested very well, and eventually ten o'clock, at long last, crawled 'Pole, Pole' into the present. There was a background noise of low-level chatter so

I assumed that none of the group had managed much, if any, sleep. I now had a good hour in which to layer-up, hopefully in the right order.

The loudest noise was coming from the porters' tents where these amazing people were beginning to prepare our breakfasts.

As for my TOE index? Well, the hike had been steep at times but it was short. The landscape was magnificent and the sun had shone all day. Despite having to take *Imodium*, I felt fine. My frame of mind was really positive and I was 'high' - in every sense of the word - on the addictive breathlessness at this altitude. So, a rather easy and enjoyable 4 out 10... man!

Chapter 11 – Day 7. The big one

Strictly speaking, of course, it wasn't tomorrow yet but still today as we all slowly assembled in the mess tent at 23:00 for breakfast. There was very little said as we were served weak hot drinks and warm comforting porridge. There was a palpable nervous uncertainty pervading the spartan air.

It wasn't a pleasant experience at all. It wasn't tangible like the headaches and diarrhoea and other conditions attributed to high altitude. This was something without a focal point that loitered ominously in the shadows of subconsciousness, constantly nagging and taunting. It would, I was sure, disperse the instant after departure for the summit.

Thankfully, I had no headache whatsoever, but I did take a couple of *Imodium* tablets and also, as a last-minute decision, prophylactically swallowed a *Diamox* pill.

At just before midnight the moment finally arrived. With all of us layered-up as never before, wearing hats that comprehensively covered ears and eyebrows, and with headtorches constantly blinding vision, it was quite tricky to tell who was who. What was certain, though, was that our group appeared like a gathering of anxious Michelin men stood uncomfortably close to a raging bonfire.

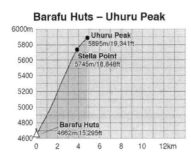

Although I hadn't planned it in advance, our summit night was taking place during a full moon. Trips during such cosmic events are quite popular apparently. Remarkably though, it was also a lunar eclipse so artificial lighting was initially required.

With one or two final unnecessary nervous adjustments of straps, laces, clothing and headtorch but definitely no farting, I was ready. Asim led us off and I intentionally took up a position at the very back of our group of eight with only one guide behind me; I think it was Naiman.

It was a truly awful start for me! By the time we'd barely reached the far end of the camp, coupled with only a few moments of gaining rather rapid ascent, I was completely and distressingly out of breath. I knew there was no way, at all, that I could keep this pace up. Not a chance!

So, I stopped, stood with my hands helplessly on my grossly burgeoning padded hips, and simply panted until I could breathe somewhat normally again. Thankfully, Matt retreated and joined me. We had a reassuring 'team talk' and agreed that I needed to go at a pace that was comfortable for me. I simply needed to forget about everyone else in the group. It was a strategy that I had successfully employed throughout most of the week so far but, in a few careless minutes of becoming totally engrossed in the moment, I had completely ignored my own strict advice.

Following a thoroughly deserved period of quiet self-chastisement, during which I regained a normal breathing pattern, I turned to Naiman and explained that I would now be continuing at a much slower pace. He was fully supportive and maybe even, whilst not exactly impressed, pleased that I'd reached my own conclusion.

Matt, as previously mentioned, had promised to stay with me all the way on the summit attempt and that was an immense comfort and support which cannot in any way be underestimated. As I set off again, I felt mightily relieved. It wasn't so much a second chance, more a resetting of the rocky ground rules. Actually, it may have been a second chance, in hindsight. It's quite possible I could have blown everything there and then. How stupid and careless of me!

With the physical side of the challenge now neatly chained up in a vault at the back of my mind, it was time to face the mental battle. Time itself was going to be largely immaterial. It wasn't a race. It was simply a case of plodding on endlessly and tediously, ignoring all the obvious hurdles and impediments, for... well, however long it would take really.

When hiking in daylight, even on a difficult climb there's usually a horizon or summit in view to act as a focal point and goal. Quite a few of these tend to reveal themselves as false summits but, never mind, there's usually then something else to aim for.

Creeping up the slopes of Kibo, however, was an entirely different proposition. Apart from our group who, incidentally, were rapidly (by steep mountain, high-altitude standards) forging ahead and leaving me behind, I could see many distant torchlit processions far, far above me but no landmarks against a velvety black starlit sky. Absolutely nothing to aim for. Simply trudge, trudge, trudge...

With no physical focus, I discovered that it was my mental state that required complete attention. I realised that it was most important to lock away, in another deep dark dungeon of my mind, any negative thoughts that might be encircling like vultures, waiting to pounce and pick at the bones of any doubts I might entertain. So, I began to recall the positive messages and advice that I'd been offered over the past few days: "never give up" from one porter, "it's a piece of cake" from a guide with an impressive command of colloquial English, or perhaps he was simply offering me a sweet titbit. There were also all the wishes of good luck from back home, especially from the children whom I couldn't possibly let down.

After two hours of battling along a crunchy, frosty endlessly twisting switch-back path, the eclipse ended and heralded a new era of bright lunar luminosity and an opportunity to stop to switch off our headtorches.

I seized the moment to remove my rucksack and produce my 'special treat'. From research, where else? I had read that the mountain guides love *Jelly Babies* and I had travelled all the way from England with a packet of the 'bad boys' (and girls? Or are they gender-fluid?) and now offered the already-opened – ok, I may have 'sampled' one or two surreptitiously over the past few days – packet to Naiman.

Even in this unearthly light, I could sense a sparkle in his eyes. He was very happy, Matt was happy, and I'd literally bought myself some valuable breathing space. I was far too out of breath to consume such a treat myself but I felt everyone was a winner at this gelatinous juncture.

Following their satisfied chewing and me gaining some control over my oxygen intake, I managed a few swigs of cool water from the bottle then it was time to set off again. It was quite apparent that, due to the freezing cold environment, any breaks would be swift ones.

Trudge, trudge, trudge…

Having studied Physics at school, I recalled that time slows down as speed increases. It's a Universal Law, one of Einstein's many beautiful equations, and as the description suggests, applies pretty much anywhere in the known everywhere. Far be it for me to challenge the brilliant man but he certainly hadn't trudged up Kilimanjaro where, as I was painfully discovering, as time slows down so does speed. I was really quite delighted with this discovery, even though I'd probably overlooked something quite obvious.

Nevertheless, I was now looking forward to presenting R Binout's Universal Law of time and motion on a steep mountain at high altitude at the Royal Society's next meeting. I playfully decided to name it: Binout's Obvious Law Of Certain Crazy Situations, or BOLOCCS for short. It hadn't been a negative thought and, ok, it wasn't positive but it had been such fun and had amused and distracted me for a good five or six minutes… I think.

Proper, 'in yer face' tiredness was setting in now and, after a few stumbles, I stopped. I needed to get my breath back and switch on my headtorch again as I was colliding with too many low-level rocks. Looking up, I could see the now familiar torchlit processions, some of which were impossibly high up. Perhaps they were stars? Unfortunately, they weren't.

The next incident of note was someone bent double over a rock, and to be blunt, retching his guts up and, in between spilling the contents of his stomach, coughing uncontrollably in a contorted state of distress. This was not the place to stop so we 'raced' on by and I attempted not to look at the appalling distress the unfortunate chap was having to endure. I felt sure, if and when, he recovered any semblance of composure then he would be led down to camp by his attendant guide; who, no doubt, had seen it all before.

After what seemed like a very long time indeed, I thought about asking Naiman the classic kids' question from the back of the car, "Are we nearly there yet?" I even managed a chuckle to myself but realised this probably wasn't the time or place and the ironic humour might be lost in translation. Besides, I couldn't speak anyway. It was far more productive simply to take a step, then breathe, take a step, breathe, etc, etc, and repeat 'x' number of times, where 'x' is a very large number indeedy. In fact, for a useful ten minutes or so, I had developed a rather efficient routine, only broken by another stumble.

After what seemed like another very long time indeed, I played a masterstroke by stopping and offering Naiman another *Jelly Baby*, which he gladly accepted with a beaming smile.

After regaining my breath, I sucked on the Camelbak mouthpiece only to find that the water had frozen in the tube. If, at that moment, I could have sent a text home it would simply have said, "FFS" (learned, of course, from my children). Not to be deterred, I squeezed the tube and crunched a few times on the mouthpiece and eventually secured a modest flow of refreshingly cold water. It trickled over the sandpaper surface of my throat and left a pleasing, freezing trail as it sunk deeper into my digestive system.

Naiman was most keen to press on so, rather than first, satisfyingly biting the head off a *Jelly Baby*, diligently followed by nibbling its legs one-by-one, I popped the whole sweet in my mouth and glanced at my watch. It was now 03:00. Only 03:00! That would be approximately half-way to Stella Point at the crater rim, I thought to myself. Only half-way to the rim. Not even the summit. FFS. I trudged on.

And... on.

Another very long time passed before I became aware of colourful lights flashing around the periphery of my vision. They were like fairies whimsically dancing and flying around my head. Well, "Fairies Wear Boots" according to Black Sabbath, I pondered. Ozzy Osbourne was then abruptly nudged aside by WB Yeats: "Faeries, come take me out of this dull world, For I would ride with you upon the wind, Run on the top of the dishevelled tide, And dance upon the mountains like a flame."

This was now a slightly hallucinogenic phase of the ascent - a high on high - and kept me occupied for another few mind-numbing minutes. Only upon standing up straight and looking around did the booted fairies sadly disappear, to be replaced by those torchlit processions still high above.

Trudge, trudge, stumble, trudge...

Following another very long time, it soon became apparent that my face was rather close to the ground. In fact, if I'd felt that way inclined, I could have kissed or dragged my tongue along the rocks. Thoughts of fatigue and cold temporarily departed as I tried to process this predicament. It was clearly a combination of the gradient of the slope together with my climbing gait having developed into an exceptionally low stoop causing, on occasion, one or two strands of my pathetic dribble to be simultaneously attached to my mouth and the volcanic gravel.

This particular hiking technique, of arse on a level with head, won't be found in any climbing manuals but it was working for me. I was in my own little bubble, quite oblivious to anyone or anything and being this close to the ground meant I could switch off the headtorch, thereby saving the batteries and helping to preserve our planet. I so wanted to share this moment with Sir David Attenborough; I'm sure he'd have been delighted. It was a win-win situation for all concerned and also a miniscule moment that I celebrated, obviously with no great fuss, as a monumental victory in this tedious battle.

It was now a miserly 04:10.

Since the dribbling episode, another very long time passed by with very little incident other than tedium, cold, and severe exhaustion. A group of three hikers then crashed past us on the way down with an accompanying guide. Even in this light, their faces appeared worryingly dreadful, so much so that they wouldn't even have cast a reflection in a mirror. Only them being confronted with a clove of garlic embedded with a protruding crucifix would have worsened their harrowing demeanour.

It was evident that they had failed in their attempt. In a terribly warped way, for which I now apologise, this awful event helped me. I was well aware that the summit success rate for this mountain was in the region of 80%, so I reasoned that my chances would improve the more desperate people we might encounter on their way down. I'm not proud of this and more than anything, what with us losing both Dougie and Steve, I genuinely wanted all eight of us to reach Uhuru Peak.

Yet another very long time elapsed during which I had entered a padded cell within my protective bubble. I had successfully released my thoughts to meander wherever they so desired on the condition that they did not focus on the immediate state of affairs.

If I hadn't been before, I was now acutely truly aware that the challenge was both physical and mental; a malicious and venomous attack on two fronts. However, I had huge faith in my mental capacity. I had made a pact with the devil in me that, if it came to it, I would leave nothing whatsoever on the mountain. My mind games would protect me from any physical limitations and would enable me to simply keep placing one foot in front of the other, no matter what. I knew there remained a long way to go but I wasn't going to stop taking tiny steps, each one of which, was edging me inexorably ever so closer to the top. It's not a race!

My trance-like state was working well. I had no real idea of my whereabouts other than 'part of the way up Kibo' and, if my over-worked lungs had contained any air, I would have happily hummed a merry tune.

I was also aware, from looking at myself from within my bubble, that the external me had developed a swaying movement to accompany the stagger. And then I stumbled sideways and ended in a slightly dazed and crumpled position, possibly cushioned in Nigella's bosom. I had no idea whether I was hurt and before I could evaluate quite what had happened, Matt and Naiman were by my side.

Matt reached for my water bottle and passed it to me. I answered a couple of questions from Naiman but have no recall of what he had asked. He helped me to my wobbly feet and stared deep into my eyes, penetrating the very depths of my being. I got the gist of what he was up to (I'd experienced something similar at school when the PE master had checked me over after falling on my head) and attempted to peer cheerfully back at him from inside my bubble, sending him a subliminal message that I was absolutely fine, in tip-top condition in fact, and definitely ready to proceed. I possibly looked like a punch-drunk boxer being inspected by the referee following a knock-down... but without the shorts and gumshield, and, if I'm honest, the physique.

"I take your rucksack now," he said softly. I was stunned, breathless with astonishment - ok, I was breathless anyway. Being stubborn and proud, I immediately declined his offer with a slightly dismissing and inebriated-looking wave of my bandaged hand and a smile - ok, perhaps drool and grimace, with a bit of dribble thrown in for effect.

Naiman firmly replied, "No, I take your rucksack, you are struggling." Even under these circumstances, I realised it was a rhetorical statement and recalled that the guides' instructions are not to be questioned. For a moment I was ever so slightly devastated. I felt as though I had failed. Game over. In fact, we might as well all go back down to camp now.

But, as I handed over my rucksack I felt as though a weight had been lifted from my shoulders - let's be honest, there's no need to add a clever comment to that. It was now 05:30 as we headed off again.

After only a short period of time, maybe fifteen minutes, the sky began to lose its black complexion and a deep purple hue was beginning to elbow its way onto the celestial scene. It was now, at last, thankfully, possible to see the crater rim; a dark silhouette against a lightening sky.

Naiman, now carrying two rucksacks, made light work of a section of large rocks with the agility of a mountain goat. It was a remarkable sight as I struggled to appear anywhere near as equally light-footed. I felt ever so slightly inadequate and pathetic.

For the final two hundred feet or so there was a lung-bursting scramble up a scree slope. And, for half an hour, with the crater rim tantalisingly close, it was three steps forward and two back as arms, hands, legs and knees were all employed in a most inelegant and ungainly final surge. Did I care? Nope. There were no marks on offer for style.

But finally, triumphantly, and to huge relief Naiman, Matt and myself made it to the reasonably flat crater rim of Kibo at Stella Point. Standing at 5,745 metres (18,848 feet) it was the highest I'd ever been on foot or, strictly speaking at this very moment, hands and knees. Incidentally, Everest Base Camp is at a height of 5,364 metres (17,598 feet).

Almost immediately, we met up with the rest of the team: Asim, two more assistant guides and the six remaining members of the group. They were all neatly positioned behind a huge lump of rock which provided a cosy shelter from the cold wind.

I was warned not to sit in a pool of sick which had only just been deposited by Bob and was still steaming in the icy cold air. How nice. But, yet again, Boring Bob was proving to be anything but. We all embraced one another, realising that this in itself was a major achievement and soon the guides brought round hot tea. It was, as I'd expected, weak and was also, just like Bob's puke, steaming but eminently more appealing.

I was very surprised to learn that the others had only been there for a few moments. I really did believe I would have been a good twenty or thirty minutes behind them such was the exceptionally pedestrian nature of my own progress. But here we all were together, now slurping on a hot drink to the beautifully glowing backdrop of an emerging African sunrise.

In my slightly bewildered state I attempted to sit and make sense of... well, everything really. If I had had a breath it would quickly have been taken away by the complex nature of this surreal situation. Here I was, sat on a crater rim of a volcano, having taken six days to climb to this point, at a ridiculous height and drinking a cup of tea next to some vomit. For one moment it seemed so eccentric in a typically English sort of way. Commencing a game of cricket seemed the next obvious thing to do. I hadn't brought my medium-sized box though.

As purples advanced into blues, an orange glow soon appeared on the horizon and then a brilliant, dazzling explosion announced the arrival of the sun at around 06:15. A new day, which for us had started last night, was beginning in earnest. It brought with it a deep, instinctive sense of optimism. Not only that, but I now knew where East was.

I could have sat here all day. OK, I was totally shattered and struggling with the lack of air but I really was most chilled and content here at Stella Point. The serenity of the circumstances reminded me so closely of the sensation following one of those long winter hikes on a bitterly cold day and then supping a pint of rich, dark ale – 'Old Farter' seemed appropriate – while thawing out in front of a roaring fire in a cosy, stone-floored pub.

Before I could order my pint, our plastic mugs were efficiently gathered up and Asim roused us to our feet for the final push.

A certificate can be awarded *simply* for getting this far. However, the official document that everyone desires most of all bears the printed words 'Uhuru Peak' and not 'Stella Point'.

All that now remained was a climb of 150 metres (493 feet) across a fraction over half a mile of crater rim. At sea-level, or any reasonable level really, that might take around fifteen to twenty minutes. So, making allowances for the current and unfamiliar conditions, I mentally prepared myself for a moderately gentle forty-five-minute stroll to the top.

Having been reinvigorated by the brief rest and hot weak tea I asked Naiman for my rucksack back. It was a matter of pride. Once again, he looked penetratingly deep inside me rather than at me and then, fully satisfied with my well-being, he handed it over. I must have passed his test, I thought to myself, as I wandered slightly aimlessly to the back of the group. What a great boost to my confidence and morale. And, with thirty years of intent, five months of intensive training, six days of, at times, extremely challenging circumstances, six hours of tedious torture, and thoughts of dear friends and family thousands of miles away all flooding and mixing around in my bemused and eager mind, I began to cry. I couldn't help myself. It arrived unannounced from an uncharted recess inside me, a secret emotional hideaway that I had been unaware of until then. It was a deeply surprising, shocking, personal visceral experience yet wonderfully uplifting. Perhaps it was a gargantuan release of some kind? Fortunately, no one witnessed this and my awkward-Englishman-abroad self abruptly regained a modicum of composure. "We'll have none of that nonsense," I scolded myself. It was a complacent and presumptuous error and, as if to emphasise the point, an enormous cracking noise from the nearby giant Rebmann Glacier quickly brought me to my senses. The final piece of my journey was indeed within my grasp but the mountain would not give up its honour without this one final challenge.

I imagined that it might be easy for keen, overenthusiastic adventurers to go rushing off at this point and perhaps jeopardise their whole trip.

Thankfully for me, though, it was only possible to shuffle along at an unbelievably pedestrian pace. The lack of air, whilst proving debilitating, was also, almost sympathetically, acting as a high-altitude speed-limiter and I was still elatedly wallowing in the intoxicating effect it was having on me. So wonderfully existential. It provided the opportunity to really appreciate the surroundings: the huge, blindingly white presence of the glacier on the left, the rocky, snow-clad trail ahead of us, and the vast, frozen, circular crater on the right. And, the being, that was me, found himself slap bang in the middle of it all, immersed, in the third person, in all of this surreal craziness. How on Earth had he got there? What on Earth was he doing there?

Every few steps we were greeted by triumphant trekkers returning from the summit. "It's just over the next ridge", "It's only five minutes away", were the popular, well-meant snippets of advice. I quickly learned to ignore these well-wishers, as false summit led to a succession of false summits and five minutes stretched ever so slowly towards half an hour, and still there was no end to this final unanticipated twist of torment.

Eventually, though, and following nearly an hour and a quarter of meandering and wishful thinking, we saw a group of people approximately two hundred yards away. And, behind them, we saw it - the famous, unremarkable, ramshackle timber slats that identify Uhuru Peak, the true top of Kibo, the ultimate lofty sanctuary of the entire African continent.

I'd like to announce that I broke out into a *Chariots of Fire* sprint to embrace my prize but that would not only have been foolhardy, it was also anatomically impossible. Instead, I continued my undignified yet effective trudge, mouth wide open and possibly dribbling again, relentlessly towards the group of ecstatic and relieved summiteers. I was soon to join them - that, at long last, was an absolute certainty now!

With almost spiritual reverence, we delicately approached as if not wanting to risk scaring it away and, as planned, Matt and I touched the sign together. We'd only gone and made it! Who'd have thought? This monumental achievement was in no small measure down to the fact that he'd remained with me *all* the way on that final summit attempt. We shook hands with a relieved smile and then embraced. Wow, we'd really done it! A most special of special moments! Live it, experience it, remember it, treasure it for ever!

Asim was clearly a master of the summit etiquette and had soon presented us with the space and opportunity for our group, and our group alone, to take all the necessary souvenir photographs in an orderly and unhurried way. Following such a momentous and free-spirited achievement, this was a more choreographed and almost crass part of the proceedings. However, once back at home, we all knew that these pictures would be the ideal catalysts with which to prompt many happy precious memories of a once-in-a-lifetime achievement.

And so, following the mandatory stage-managed photos, I removed myself from the melee. Only a few feet away was sufficient. I stood there in quiet self-congratulatory contemplation. At 5,895 metres (19,341 feet, or 13.87 WBs) it was the highest I'd ever been on foot. The sense of achievement of what was, by my standards, a ludicrously ambitious and by no means certain goal engulfed me with every conceivable inspirational and joyous emotion imaginable.

For that brief moment, I was invincible, arguably the greatest explorer within the 27-49 demographic age group, of the modern era, perhaps of any era. The sky was a devastating spectrum of dynamic blues, the volcanic dust which lay around my feet was the most vibrant lunar grey I'd ever seen, the clouds, which were shading the mere mortals at ground level, were far below us, and the panoramic horizon in the faraway misty distance was indeed, as I'd read, not straight but ever so slightly curved. The summit of Africa truly was an extraordinarily magnificent and spiritual haven on Earth. Incredibly, I'd made it and I surrendered myself to allow this euphoric moment to permeate my exhausted wreck of mind and body. Exhausted, yes, but never, ever more alive!

Matt and myself then removed ourselves further away from the bustling summit sign, found a spot to allow some (heavy) breathing space, sat down together and purveyed all before us. It was a perfect opportunity to fully appreciate the scenery. We then rummaged for our mobile phones and composed a short text each, confirming that we'd succeeded. I have no idea if the messages were immediately 'sent' though. Anyway, there was far, far, far too much to savour right here and right now.

Typically, we both then had a desire to go and explore the crater and, instinctively, we both knew that only one of us would have been capable. However, with the rest of our group having now departed, Asim gathered the two of us together and we began the leisurely stroll back along the rim now, thankfully, in a downwards direction.

But then, we had to turn around again. Matt had just recalled his promise to the retailer from where he'd bought our cosy 5-season sleeping bags. After a bit of faffing around, and a fully warranted FFS, I eventually took a couple of photos of Matt holding a branded carrier bag in front of the summit sign. Anything else Matt? There wasn't and we confidently departed.

I was highly tiddly now through both the lack of oxygen as well as a strange feeling of tranquil elation. And, with a beaming glacier-sized smile I turned to Asim and told him that I loved him. Fortunately, I resisted the temptation to take the relationship a step further by confessing that I wanted to move in with him and start a family. Besides, it would have been a tad awkward the following morning. Instead, Asim simply laughed and put his arm around me. Perhaps he'd heard it all before.

It was now our turn to greet oncoming would-be summiteers with encouraging words as we casually strode towards Stella Point. Once there, it was possible to see the whole extent of the route we'd slogged and struggled up all those hours ago. It was immediately apparent that it had been a far better proposition to have made the ascent in darkness; Barafu Huts camp, some four thousand feet below, seemed impossibly out of reach, especially in these rarified conditions.

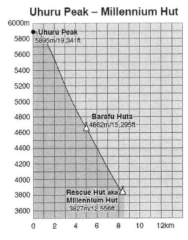

The way down from here was slightly different from the route up in that it was predominantly scree-based to begin with. This provided the opportunity to take large, lumbering steps rather like running down a sand dune.

It was a blessed relief to begin with and in such marked contrast to the endless trudging on the parallel route up. However, after half an hour, my boots had filled up with coarse volcanic debris and my legs and knees were beginning to feel fatigued and, on top of all that, I was sweating quite profusely; still wearing the original nine layers!

It came as no surprise when I soon went tumbling arse over tit, performing several rotations, maybe involving a pike and a tuck, and ending up in a sprawling, giggling heap. Matt accused me of attention-seeking. My mind briefly, very briefly, pondered *the* poles back down at camp!

Being ever so slightly dazed, I took a few moments to recompose myself, shed four layers of clothing and emptied my boots, at which point I could sense the development of a few nasty blisters - the first of the week. I sat and wondered what the collective noun for blisters was - a 'brood of blisters'? - before lolloping uncontrollably down the dusty slopes once more. What had initially been fun was quickly metamorphosing into an unforeseen *Hammer Hike of Downhill Horrors*.

Eventually, as we approached camp, the slopes levelled out and it was, at long last, possible to walk with a hint of normality. Soon, Matt and I were met by two porters just on the outskirts of camp and one of them, a young lad, relieved me of my rucksack and escorted us back to our tent. I hadn't expected this 'welcome home' greeting but it was hugely appreciated, if only, to enable us the quickest passage to having a deserved rest.

Following ten hours of torture, drudgery, jubilation and severe physical and mental fatigue I'm not convinced I could have easily found our way back through the mini tented village. I'd probably have entered the first tent we came to, empty or not, and collapsed in a helpless heap.

I had absolutely, positively, without any doubt, nothing left in reserve whatsoever. Whatever I had had, had most certainly been left on Kibo (together with the word 'had' hopefully). I was 'out on my feet' and therefore could only manage a pathetic crawl into the tent, fully believing I'd never been so exhausted in my life. I certainly didn't have the energy to attempt to recall such a time, which would have been pointless anyway, as I hadn't ever been this tired - had I already mentioned that? A knacker's yard would have rejected me. Instead, I sat in the 'porch' and focussed on removing my boots to inspect the damage.

As was the case at this altitude of *just* 4,662 metres (15,295 feet) it was only possible to attend to one foot at a time before a breather was required. My right foot had an impressive festering brood of three burst blisters. I allowed them to throb and sting in the cool sun-drenched air while I brooded over my other foot. Five minutes later, my left foot revealed similar damage; again, burst and smudged all over their host toes. Blimey, they smarted!

I had anticipated blisters but not on this cataclysmic scale. Top layers of skin had been brutally ripped and torn out of position and spread out in a haphazard fashion leaving behind tender weeping circles of pink flesh. Blimey, they stung! The redeeming fact of having six extremely painful blisters was that no single one could claim the spotlight of sensory perception. Consequently, the focus of pain was constantly moving. Well, that was comforting, I convinced myself. I set about nursing the festering, brooding mess. Some of the skin was neatly positioned back over their weeping craters before tentatively applying blister plasters. Other shreds of flesh were simply left in situ as they were either far too painful to rip off completely or in such a poor condition that they wouldn't have sufficiently covered the wounds that they had deserted.

Soon after admiring the handiwork on my feet, Asim announced that it was time to leave Barafu and head down to Millennium Hut. What! Come on! Given the choice, I would have preferred to have stayed and slept for a month but as it definitely wasn't an option I very carefully pulled on my socks and gently squeezed my swollen feet, blisters and blister plasters into my boots and tentatively stood up. Oooh the sharp searing pain! My grotesque grimace would have ensured me a podium finish at the World Gurning Championships. In a Stephen Redgrave-like declaration, I immediately announced to Matt that I would never ever go near a fucking mountain ever again! Next year, we would be taking up embroidery.

The descent to the next camp was 835 metres (2,739 feet) and along a route of 3½km (just over 2 miles), making it yet another blister-nurturing excursion. Fortunately, I had very little damage-free skin left remaining on my feet to blister. Such was the pain, though, that I took as many paracetamol tablets as were permitted on the guidelines and hobbled off with Matt, who was extraordinarily perky, seemingly not in the least bit tired, and whose blisters numbered zero. A six-nil victory to me was no cause for celebration. Yes, everyone else in our group was tired to varying degrees but I was the only one with blisters. I certainly had sufficient to share around.

The route down did not retrace any footsteps and therefore the new scenery provided a reasonable level of distraction from the pain of the blisters - had I mentioned my blisters?

We soon passed a couple of metal-framed trollies, similar to those in a DIY store but with only one wheel. These unicycled-trolley-stretchers (I don't for one second think that's their actual name) are designed to take a person as quickly as possible to lower altitudes in the case of a medical emergency. It would, undoubtedly, be an extremely bumpy ride to safety.

Asim, with that familiar glint in his eyes and knowing exactly what was going through my mind at that very moment, confirmed that blisters were not classed as a medical emergency. So, I next pretended to pass out but he was having none of it. Maybe I could have painted my lips blue, I thought. We all plodded on.

Back home in the UK, my summit-confirming text had obviously been received and word was circulating.

On 2 June 1953 it was Coronation Day for Queen Elizabeth II and, not only that, but news of the first conquest of Everest hit the front pages of Britain's newspapers. "Be proud of Britain on this day, Coronation Day... All this - and Everest Too" reported the *Daily Express*.

My news, whilst not making the front pages, was, though, enthusiastically announced by a teaching assistant (an excitable person and very dear friend) who burst into the school canteen and proclaimed to my two children, and therefore the rest of the school too, that I'd made it. Knowing my kids, who do not like the limelight or any unnecessary attention, I'm sure they felt nothing but complete and utter embarrassment. But hey, that's part of a Dad's job description.

Finally, at around 14:30, we reached Millennium Hut camp and sat on a bench. Only three hours ago I had been the most tired, weary, exhausted, worn out, drained, bushed and fatigued than at any other moment in my life... times three. It was in fact the most tired any human being had ever been in the history of humans being tired. Now, however, I was all of that, plus one! A World Record!

Amazingly, this camp had a 'shop'! However, at a blistering forty feet away, it was too far even for me – a recently recognised Record Breaker - to reach. Matt casually sauntered over and soon returned with a couple of cans of Coke. In that moment his already unsurmountable position of 'best hiking mate ever in the whole world' went up a notch, only to be swiftly revoked as he consumed his first can and then immediately started on his second. What a complete... and then, with a huge grin, he handed me two cans from his pocket.

I'd given up these teeth-rotting 'treats' years ago but was more than happy to indulge in this delight on this one special occasion. Following days of consuming boiled and sterilised water, this cool sparkling black nectar was a most unexpected naughty-but-nice delight. With no visible retail competition in the camp, I dreaded to think how much they'd cost. I never did find out.

Following a great deal of satisfying belching, all I longed for now was a lie down. The pain of my feet was only equalled by my absolute need for rest. After locating our tent and realising the toilet facilities were far too far away for someone in my wretched condition, I had a wee beside a neighbouring bush, crawled inside the tent and removed my boots. It's possible I was already in the very deepest of sleeps before I'd gingerly manoeuvred myself into my sleeping bag and...

Chapter 12 – Day 8. Running Water

... the next thing I knew, it was tomorrow!

As for the previous day's TOE index? Well, we'd first of all ascended 1,233 metres (4,046 feet) to reach Uhuru Peak and then followed up with a descent of 2,068 metres (6,785 feet) in approximately fourteen and a half hours. In an attempt to break the world record for understatements, I regarded that feat as somewhat challenging as my own poor feet bore witness to. So, 17 out of 10 would seem reasonable. Had I mentioned the extreme fatigue and agonizingly painful blisters?

I don't know whether it was the pre-dawn light gently tickling my senses that woke me up or my mahoosive bladder which had all too obviously reached 'full'. Either way, the neighbouring bush took another soaking I do not usually make a habit out of relieving myself over bushes. However, it was such a relief to have to walk only a few paces and the steaming hot, dark brown urine in the chilly morning air added an attractive ethereal misty touch to proceedings. The short journey in my socks, however, was of sufficient distance to remind me that my blisters were once again loudly attention-seeking. I resisted, though, intending instead to have a proper look once in the relative comfort of our lodge some time later that day.

Back in the tent, Matt brought me up to date with the previous night's activities. First of all, he took great delight in telling me that I'd been in such a deep sleep that I'd failed to notice when a baboon had entered our tent, fondled my balls and given me a blowjob. "Oh haha," I thought after, first, having a quick peek 'down below' to check for any telltale signs of such activity. Not, I hasten to add, that I'd have any idea what 'telltale' signs to look for following such an act from a baboon. A Colobus monkey on the other hand... but 'what goes on in the jungle stays in the jungle'!

It had been the final night on the mountain and, as is the custom on such a trip, the group, in my absence, had all agreed the varying levels of tips, according to the job they did, for the porters, chef, assistant guides and head guide. Matt, knowing me so well, appreciated that I had needed sleep (and possibly a blowjob) more than anything else and that I'd be perfectly happy to go along with the tips decided upon.

It had been overwhelmingly humbling to see the effort, care and consideration that these people had displayed at *all* times in helping us achieve our, in the grand scheme of life's struggles, relatively superficial ambition. Not only that, one or two of them had attire that I wouldn't have dreamt of wearing in a Mediterranean holiday resort in high summer let alone in these, at times, highly inhospitable conditions. Their singing and huge smiles could lift a low and flagging disposition in an instant. Some had carried loads of up to 30kg and not one had the stocky, tree-trunked leg-build of a rugby prop-forward. In fact, they mostly resembled those lithe, free-spirited kids kicking a football around on Copacabana Beach.

It is because of their immense, unconditional support, that anyone who has ever embarked upon such a trip is compelled to offer as large a tip as possible and is still left wishing they could give more; we were certainly no different.

It is also an opportunity to leave behind whatever gear you no longer have a need for. For me, the bloody walking poles (one of which, bizarrely, was covered in dark chocolate) were an obvious donation. I happily deposited several warm, almost brand new fleeces into a collection bag too.

Despite a gruelling few days, it was a most cheerful breakfast during which wounds and ailments were compared but in a light-hearted manner. Bob had won the 'Vomit Cup' but I thrashed everyone to lift the 'Blister Trophy' as well as the 'Knackered Tankard'. I thought I was deserving of some nice crystal too for my life-threatening hand flesh wound, now wrapped in a filthy, volcanic dust-impregnated bedraggled bandage. For ladies who preferred their men rough, tough, blistered and battered, I was surely their ultimate dream? There was little evidence of a queue forming though. Well, none at all, actually.

Following breakfast, it was then time for the customary tipping ceremony. This is a *key* feature of any Kilimanjaro trek and one to be cherished. It is viewed as an obligatory act but should be regarded as a joyful celebration for everyone involved: head guide, assistant guides, porters, chef and hikers. The money given, goes directly to the support team, and forms a significant part of their income. So, for the first time since meeting our support team a week ago, this was one final opportunity to see them all together again and a time to thank them for their incredible help.

Andy and Mike handed out the financial rewards which were announced by Asim to fervent, appreciative and reciprocated applause from *everyone* as each member of the team came forward to receive their tip. They all appeared genuinely pleased and touched.

Tips awarded, spontaneous clapping then broke-out amongst the support team, who were proudly bunched in a big group facing us and now swaying from side to side in unison. It signalled the start of two traditional songs: 'Kilimanjaro' and 'Hakuna Matata'. Yes, we'd heard snippets of these tunes throughout the trip sung by the porters. This, though, was the proper full-on performance. They each sung with verve and gusto plucked from their hearts. There was a carnival atmosphere, jubilant and very moving. Once again, their infectious smiles could not fail to warm the coldest heart. And yes, a huge lump in my throat preceded an uncontrollable watering of my eyes. I was slightly self-conscious about my latest display drawn from a well of emotion and, consequently, didn't look around at my fellow group members. However, I'm sure I wasn't alone in feeling and reacting this way. It was sad when the celebrations eventually ended but it had been a fitting way to say goodbye.

The only thing remaining was to depart Millennium Camp and leave the Kilimanjaro National Park; a landscape of bewildering variety and challenging contrasts. So, the party was over but we weren't going our separate ways, we were all leaving together. Tired minds and bodies packed rucksacks for one final time. The mood was one of relief but also permeated with immense pride. Happy chatter, reflecting our recent personal triumphs quickly flowed.

For me, not only was there a small amount of emotional reluctance to set off, but I also had those bloody unbearable blisters to contend with. They really were very painful indeed and I'd have happily exchanged them for a hornet's sting in each of my eyeballs. Consequently, Matt and myself took our time, staying at the very back of the group with only assistant guide, Joshua, for company.

We hadn't been given a briefing for this final day's trek. I certainly hadn't researched it. I presumed it was all downhill and that's all I needed to know. Given what we'd been through during the past week, this section seemed superfluous.

Every now and then, we glanced back over our shoulders to savour final fleeting glimpses of the gleaming white mountain top. Even though it appeared impossibly far away Matt stated that he could quite easily have gone back up again to the summit after breakfast that morning, and I knew he wasn't kidding either. I, meanwhile, was still steadfastly maintaining that this was my last time *ever* on a mountain. No question, whatsoever!

Finally, the well-defined footpath became so shrouded in tall tropical trees that Kibo was invisible to us. A dear, respected friend but brutal foe had vanished and, to be honest, I missed it very deeply. It had been the absolute focal point of my life for a week following five tough months of training and preparation. I realised that I'd formed an emotional bond with a lump of volcanic rock. Is it a similar feeling as that of, say, a footballer when they hang up their boots for the final time?

With exceptionally painful feet, the trek now became torture and tedious. My thoughts were already racing ahead to a long, hot shower and a change of clothing. Volcanic dust had settled absolutely everywhere: under fingernails, up nostrils, in eyes and ears, and was inhabiting most other bodily crevices too. My t-shirt reeked with old, stale sweat and my underpants, given half the chance, could have walked down by themselves. I wasn't even sure they were worth taking home to put through the 'industrial' wash setting. They might not even have been permitted through UK customs. Any keen, alert sniffer hound would have regarded them as the dog's bollocks. I considered them a dire health risk and most certainly would not have allowed them into the country had I been one of those members of staff wearing the fearsome rubber gloves.

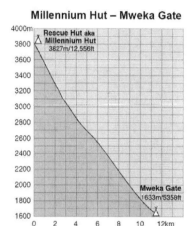

By now, Colobus monkeys were noisily announcing their presence high up in the jungle canopy. We stopped for a break under an enormous tree. At ground level, its dark brown gnarled trunk must have been fifteen feet in diameter. Joshua described this monstrous specimen as the 'medicine tree'. It had a plentiful supply of peeling brown bark which, apparently, was good for stomach ailments. The continued stinging sensation trapped within my boots prompted me to look around for the 'blister tree'.

After a long and tedious downhill slog, taking approximately five hours, we finally stumbled into the buildings at Mweka Gate, at the edge of the National Park, in order to complete the administrative formalities.

Asim oversaw proceedings to ensure all the correct details had been entered onto our certificates before we all officially exited the park with undue fuss and entered the outside world.

I wasn't expecting a welcoming party of dignitaries, TV cameras, reporters, balloons, live music, tombolas and a splat-a-rat stall, consequently I wasn't in the slightest bit disappointed. It was, in fact, a very low-key exit.

191

Apart from a few vendors of touristy tat and tired trekkers, there was little else happening. I did have a quick browse through the impressive artwork and t-shirts on sale but wasn't really in the right frame of mind for retail therapy. How on Earth was it possible to have captured the sights, sounds, smells, highs and lows of the past week on a t-shirt as a memento? Buying everything on sale, apart from being utterly stupid, could not have come close to reflecting the myriad experiences. And besides, I'd taken plenty of photos and kept a diary - maybe I'd write a book one day...

I glanced at an official park sign which stated it was 22½km (14 miles) and 18 hours to Uhuru Peak from there. It was largely irrelevant, though, as I'd been there, done it, seen it, and not bought the t-shirt.

Anyway, I'd officially retired from mountains now. Today's route, and the final part of the whole trek, had been a somewhat cruel descent of 2,194 metres (7,198 feet) along a distance of some 12 kilometres (7½ miles). It had been, literally, all downhill, following achieving our goal the previous day when a helicopter ride back to the lodge would have been a far kinder ending, Instead, I'd had to endure the completely unanticipated sensation of walking on broken glass with salt being rubbed into open weeping wounds.

It had certainly been a tough finish and my final TOE index came in at 11 out of 10. This presented a neat symmetry for it exactly matched the number of blisters I felt I was now carrying.

Not surprisingly, after rapidly descending 4,262 metres (13,983 feet) from the summit within the space of twenty-nine hours - a large part of which I'd actually been asleep in my tent - my knees, thighs and eleven smarting blisters really had, genuinely, had enough now... and so had I.

With everyone now on the outside of the park, we made the short, and unaccustomed, flat walk into Mweka village for a lunch stop and one final gathering with Asim and the assistant guides.

The talk was trivial in the warm sunshine as we reflected on *the* most memorable trip any of us had ever been on. As our minibus arrived, I quickly sought out Naiman. He had looked after me so caringly, sympathetically and lovingly on the summit night. It was still crystal clear in my mind. I wanted to get this special, deeply personal show of appreciation right. So, I handed him a significant tip, babbled an impulsive heartfelt appreciation, then gave him an almighty hug… and asked if he was carrying any blister plasters. Nah, not really. That would have spoiled a very special moment.

As I relinquished the embrace, we looked each other in the eye with a knowing expression and huge respect, and it must be said, ever so slightly tearfully. Gosh, I loved him too - what would Asim think? I'll never forget Naiman's warm, deep brown eyes and sunshine smile.

Only Asim now remained with the group. He would return to the lodge with us where, maybe, I'd have to confess my feelings that I'd developed towards one of his assistant guides.

The journey back to the lodge provided quiet time for wistful reflection in familiar surroundings. We were in our original minibus and the cracked windscreen still hadn't been fixed. The only obvious difference was that the pungent waft of body odour aroma had matured nicely like a blue cheese or eau-de-'long-drop' toilette ™.

The blurry scenery flashed by as my unfocused eyes allowed my mind to recall treasured moments during the past week. And then, for the first time, I began to fully appreciate that I'd really done it! Years of idle talk, months of training, days of research and hours of planning had finally, at long long last, perfectly come to fruition. I'd never doubted I would succeed. (Yeah, right!) With the exception of my first kiss, aged five-and-a-half, with 'Mad Mandy' Crankshaw (who had been an imposing, knee-knocking eight months my senior) it was undoubtedly my biggest sense of achievement ever.

My trance-like state was interrupted the moment the minibus left the road and headed up the bumpy track, signalling we were only a few hundred yards away from our final destination for the day: the complex where we'd spent the first day.

Matt and I were allocated the very same chalet we'd stayed in previously. A nice touch of synchronicity, I thought, but what of the monstrous flappy moth, whining mosquito, voyeuristic gecko and 'the thing' in the thatch?

After collecting our valuables from reception, which we'd left behind before setting off up the mountain, we headed off discussing who would shower first. I was happy to concede that particular luxury as I *really* did need to examine my blisters before anything else.

Thankfully, the electricity was on so while Matt basked in a steaming hot shower, I very cautiously peeled off my socks praying that no toes would become detached in the process.

Certainly, my feet were far less painful than the previous day but they were both a complete mashup of misplaced skin, plasters, pink weepy bits, all attractively finished off with a random sprinkling of volcanic dust; even someone with a perverted foot fetish would have baulked at the sight.

I think the concept behind 'blister' plasters is that they merge with the skin forming an indistinguishable layer which later, hopefully, all falls off naturally leaving a perfectly healed wound. But both my feet were in a right mess and they begged me to do something, anything. Surely, I couldn't leave them like that? Should I pick at the dead bits? Pull at loose ends? Perform some general tidying up?

It was tempting to reach for my penknife for remedial inspiration. I'd bought it as a special treat during my training period earlier in the year but had only used one of the blades in amongst the umpteen tools available - since you ask, to slice an apple in a rugged, manly way. It was a bit of shame, really, as I'd had every intention of using each and every one of them for whittling wooden spears and figurines, skinning rabbits, gutting fish, filing my nails, building canoes and life-saving shelters and, as every intrepid explorer should do, sawing off a trapped limb. And, once back to safety, I would then open a celebratory bottle of wine with the small and lethally difficult-to-use corkscrew. However, even that seemed unlikely as most of my favourite whites now came with screw-tops.

Perhaps, though, this was now an opportunity to use the scissors or that funny spikey pick-like implement that's normally reserved for digging stones out of horses' hoofs. I really wasn't quite sure what to do next. Consequently, as a last resort, it was time to read the instructions on the blister plaster box.

How enlightening. I should have cleaned and dried my skin *before* use. I seemed to recall rubbing my grubby hands on my dusty trousers before applying the plasters on not totally pristine feet. But, given the circumstances, I'm sure my resourceful 'scrub up' would have been sufficient. Once on, they should then be "left in place until they start to detach, which could take up to several days". So, my conclusion was to take no further action. I was more than happy with that. It very closely followed my mantra of: if you leave something long enough it will surely go away... or drop off.

The next task was to empty the contents of my rucksack and kit bag all over the floor and sort into 'clean', 'dirty', 'filthy', 'thoroughly rancid' and 'to be condemned' piles. The latter was thrown straight into a bin and the tiny 'clean' section indicated what I had left to wear in order to get home. The rest was abruptly stuffed back into my kit bag. Job done!

The shower that followed was absolute, unadulterated bliss. As I allowed the hot cleansing water to seep deeply into every grimy pore, I pictured myself in a bikini on a hot tropical island, seductively caressing my body, applying coconut oil and tucking into a *Bounty* bar. Yep, all a bit weird really. It's probably just as well I haven't confessed these intimate details to anyone. Anyway, afterwards it was such a huge relief to be clean again and, it has to be added, not wearing a rather fetching two-piece ladies' swimsuit.

Neither Matt nor myself are the types to sit around a pool and, as we'd flown thousands of miles to get here and probably wouldn't ever return, we agreed it was time to explore the nearest town and appreciate the local culture. So, we found Asim, who made a quick phone call, and within forty minutes the three of us plus a driver were heading off to the nearest town of Arusha. It's located approximately 50km (30 miles) to the west of Kilimanjaro Airport with a population of around 400,000 and features an impressive backdrop of the nearby Mount Meru.

The wonderful feeling of being clean and fresh soon dissipated as we sat in the back of a stuffy car devoid of air conditioning. I doubt the vehicle even had an MOT. It must have clocked-up well over two hundred thousand miles, endured several 'careful' owners but, to be fair, it possessed four wheels and was full of 'character'.

All the car's windows were wide open as we bumped and trundled along but this failed to abate the onrush of dripping armpits. As with all the locals, our driver was a happy, smiley chap and, as with all the locals, he was not in a hurry. He casually drove with one elbow permanently out of the window in the classic football manager, Harry Redknapp's pose, when being interviewed by reporters upon leaving the training ground in the comfort of his 4x4.

Our driver's other hand was occasionally on the steering wheel but found better employment by tending to his cigarette. I'd spent the best part of a week covered in volcanic dust, now it was fag ash. But hey, I wanted to experience authentic local life.

Once in the town, the first landmark of any note was the centrally-located Clock Tower. It's a rectangular, mostly brick structure, maybe 25-30 feet in height featuring... yes, a four-faced clock. By the time I'd fully clocked its appearance in the middle of a roundabout, our driver had haphazardly parked the car and we were deposited on a pavement.

Under a heavy but occasionally broken thick white cloud blanket the atmosphere was warm and sticky; rather similar to the stagnant environment now contained inside my pants.

Asim proceeded to lead us into an unremarkable café. White plastic tables were accompanied by white plastic chairs, scattered upon a white, tiled floor. The white, plastic laminated menu featured several appealing lunchtime snacks and a smiling, cheerful black waiter took our orders. I simply couldn't resist the chicken curry. I'd gone fifteen days without a curry - yes, I *was* counting - and was simply gagging for one.

By the time the bowl arrived, I was in a frenzied state of salivation. Tragically, after the first mouthful my stomach gave clear signs that it wasn't yet ready for a curry. Disappointingly, an ever so slight feeling of nausea meant I was only able to pick at the soft white rice. Matt, however, voraciously tucked into his curry and had finished in a matter of only a few minutes.

A short stroll then took us to the nearby open air Maasai Market. Asim sat down on a kerb chatting to some friends, leaving Matt and I free to explore this bustling, colourful environment. I was a little hesitant to begin with.

Twenty years previously, I'd been in the Grand Bazaar in Istanbul and experienced horrendous hassling and hustling of the highest degree. All manner of goods (mostly "nice slippers") had been forced into my hands, prices discussed and my wife fondled (not by me) before I'd had the opportunity to acclimatise to this most unfamiliar aggressive 'market mode'. Thankfully, here in Arusha, there was a much gentler, relaxed ambience.

We wandered up and down the 'avenues' of market stalls looking for gifts to take back home. There was all manner of wares and fare on display: brightly coloured 'canvas' paintings of Maasai Warriors, fearful looking spears that would be tricky to carry on to an airplane, bags, handbags and purses made from leather as well as plant-based materials, dangly earrings, vibrantly coloured bracelets, and teak carvings of classic African animals, including five-feet high giraffes - who on Earth would buy those let alone attempt to take one home? The visual experience of colour and bustle was only matched by the deep, earthy smells of the leather, parchment and wooden goods.

Yes, there was clearly some touristy tat on sale but, judging by the predominance of locals milling around, it felt like a proper piece of authentic African life to me.

Without exception, every single market stall holder greeted us with a beaming smile and no hint of overzealous sales tactics whatsoever. It was such a wonderfully friendly experience - and I hate shopping.

I had learned a few basic Swahili words, such as, 'hello', 'please' and 'thank you' and, in my usual awkward-Englishman-abroad way, tentatively used them to great effect much to the delight of the market vendors who, of course, replied to me in near-perfect English.

To this day, it never ceases to amaze me how widely spoken my mother tongue is. Native English speakers are very lucky in this regard but it's never prevented me from learning a few words of the local language during my travels. At the very least, it's the polite thing to do.

The market place had provided me with my first ever 'relaxed' opportunity to haggle over prices; an alien concept to a great deal of people from the West. However, I had been a Buyer for a well-known retailer for many years and was ready to flex my negotiating business muscle in order to squeeze every last Tanzanian shilling out of each and every transaction; and hopefully impress Lord Sugar.

That is, until, my other-self took control and realised that I would be negotiating over 'mere' pennies which, to me, was 'nothing' but may have represented a reasonable amount to these sellers. My conclusion was to enter into the sport and custom of bartering but not get too hung up on the final price. Agree a reasonable deal with a smile, a handshake and feel the love. It's my inner hippy, and I'm happy with that. Namaste.

For ease of carrying presents home, I settled on bracelets for each member of my family. Colourful, beaded ones for the 'girls' and a leather strapped one with red, yellow and green stringy 'ties' for myself. I'd been given a particularly impressive sales demonstration for the one I bought my son. It was made from black elephant tail hair which, apparently, couldn't be set alight. The seller produced a cigarette lighter and unsuccessfully attempted to burn it. I was so impressed, I bought two and then departed his 'I saw you coming' stall feeling very pleased with my purchases.

With the anxiety and pressure of having to buy presents for loved ones at home lifted, I then, stupidly, got swept away in, both, my euphoria and the whole African market experience and purchased a five-feet high beautifully carved teak giraffe. It had looked magnificent in situ and was a bargain but, upon positioning it under an armpit, I immediately began to have doubts. "You're fired!"

We then found Asim. Just for a split second, I felt sure he rolled his eyes when seeing my 'pet'. We'd thoroughly enjoyed our experience of local life but it was now time to leave Arusha and return to the lodge for the final time. Asim advised us on the level of tip to give the driver and we also handed over double that amount to our trusted guide and friend. We travelled back in the same stuffy, comfy car, only this time, the four elbows peeking out of the four fully opened windows were accompanied by a giraffe's head.

Upon arrival back at the lodge, the beers were already flowing amongst the group. Naturally it was *Kilimanjaro Premium Lager*. What else! It had been three weeks since I'd had any alcohol so I'd like to say that I savoured this cool, refreshing celebratory drink in an appreciative and leisurely fashion but, conversely, it was downed in one, closely followed by a throaty belch.

And that was it for me as far as the lager was concerned. I love my real ales back home, good old warm British beers, but lager gives me a terrible headache, especially after the tenth pint. So, I ventured into the lounge area and bought myself a bottle of chilled Pinot Grigio; it had a screw-top.

There was much laughter and reminiscing as the evening wore on but we did spare a thought for Dougie and Simon who, by now, were both back home in England and hopefully fully recovered. All the emotions experienced were recounted and relived from the safety of our lodge. The general consensus was one of utter relief that there would be no more suffering of the 'long-drop' toilets, freezing cold and headaches. Instead, it was time to cherish our combined achievement and to fart away without the fear of damaging our underwear. There is such a special bond when a group has been pushed to their absolute limits and, together, through support and friendship have conquered the toughest of tasks.

As the evening wore on and realising what a complete fool I'd been, I discretely placed my 'pet' giraffe in the lounge near the fireplace and a neat pile of logs. It looked as though it had been part of the furniture all along. It certainly was now.

Matt and I then returned to our hut at around 22:30. Not wanting the day to end, we sat on our private patio area, supped our drinks, and listened to the frenetic orchestra of nocturnal invertebrates... followed by the vertebrates.

We quietly chatted and reflected upon what we had been through. It seemed incredible that, here we were, sat under a balmy African night sky having only just conquered Kili together, as we'd planned and trained for six months ago - yep, we could call it Kili now; we'd *more* than earned that right!

It was a relaxing, calming setting, one which we thoroughly deserved following the exertions of the past few days. Even when the electricity went off - together with the unmistakable smell of a burned-to-a-crisp

200

gecko who'd recently chewed on some power cables - and we had to resort to headtorches, we still had no inclination to turn in for the night.

We could have sat there basking for hours. I think we probably did.

Chapter 13 – Day 9. Back home

Upon waking there was a feeling of reluctance, sadness and resignation. It was now a case of simply wanting to be back home without the need for the tiresome lengthy journey. Miraculously, and it took me a few hesitant moments to fully realise it, my long-standing short-sightedness had corrected itself overnight. I couldn't quite believe what had happened and asked Matt to hold up a book and test my vision.

Sure enough, his sight test revealed I could read at distance. We concluded that the miracle was most likely down to the effects of altitude and it would probably wear off in a few days' time, such was our combined ophthalmic knowledge.

The visionary miracle, in fact, lasted all of a few minutes until I discovered, during shaving, that I'd obviously gone to bed still wearing my contact lenses. I'd never, ever done that before, fully aware of stories, maybe urban myths, of contact lenses finding their way round to the back of wearers' eyes. Plus, a friend of mine once told me that he'd had an eyeball removed from its socket in order to have some 'detritus' cleared away AND, during this procedure, his detached eyeball had been swivelled around so that he was able to look back at himself! To this day, I'm still guessing as to the veracity of his account.

As for me, I certainly hadn't drunk too much the previous night so I surmised that exhaustion had led to a bypassing of the routine night-time ablutions. Oh well. Anyway, me reaching the top of Kili was my own little personal miracle.

After breakfast and farewells to the locals, it was time to depart the lodge. Whereas we had arrived independently, we were leaving as a fully-bonded group and still had a little longer in each other's company.

We returned to Kilimanjaro International Airport in the minibus with the familiar cracked windscreen. And now, *only* being a group of eight with all bags stowed away on the roof, there was noticeably more room in which to sweat and fart. I derived comfort from the fact the crack remained. Our final journey in this dear old friend. It's funny how we become attached to inanimate objects. I was slightly missing my giraffe.

We did, once again, change planes at Nairobi for the long flight back to Heathrow. However, I'd stopped writing my diary by this stage and cannot recall any detail of our long journey home; other than utter exhaustion.

Eventually, after hours of travelling and successfully reclaiming our baggage, the group swapped email addresses, phone numbers and hugs at Heathrow Arrivals lounge and went our separate ways. It had obviously been a tiring week with long-haul flights at either end. We'd also experienced many emotional goodbyes with our guides as well as two team members. Perhaps, therefore, it wasn't totally unexpected that this final farewell had been far simpler and more matter of fact. Everyone simply wanted to get home.

There are three things I'm always wary of at Arrivals: will my hold luggage have followed me, will I get stopped and searched going through 'Nothing to Declare', and will I be able to locate my car park ticket? Thankfully, all three were passed without undue fuss. That is, until I looked at that neat little space, on the car park ticket, reserved for writing down where one had parked. Bugger! So, Matt and I spent a little longer than originally anticipated in finding my car. But hey, after what we'd been through, this was merely a minor irritation.

By the time we arrived at Reading Services, we were both very hungry and in need of a good old-fashioned English breakfast. It wasn't long after 06:00 as we piled our plates high with eggs, baked beans, hash browns, mushrooms, bacon and sausages, with a glass of orange juice and a mug of hot tea on the side.

The place was pretty much deserted and we waited for quite some time at the till to pay. We even waited a little longer and still no one came to take our money so we decided to grab the sachets of tomato sauce and sit down.

We tucked in loudly and voraciously and still no one popped out of the kitchens to witness the hungry heroes' return. It's not as if we'd stuffed the food down our tops or in our pockets and dashed out. We sat there quite blatantly enjoying a large wholesome breakfast.

It was so strange being back in the UK with our 'secret mission' now accomplished. Of the few people who were in the Services, not one of them was aware of what Matt and I had just done - and I don't mean 'stolen' a breakfast each. These people, though, wouldn't *really* have understood even if we told them. Maybe it was a post-trip blues of sorts, but I sympathetically viewed these miserable-looking people, going about their miserable lives in order to eke out a miserly living, as somewhat pathetic souls. So, back to normal life. Was that it?

By 06:30 we'd finished our breakfasts, were most satisfied, and still no one had appeared to take our money. So, we departed feeling very puzzled and slightly guilty. Perhaps Reading Services might like to check their CCTV images. I have since visited on many occasions and still no one has presented me with a bill or arrested me.

Approaching my home, I practised what I was going to say to the local newspaper reporter who would be parked on my drive. However, only Mrs Binout was there but that was all that really mattered. The kids, who were at school, had placed some balloons and 'Welcome Home' bunting in the hall. What a lovely touch. I simply couldn't wait to see, hold and smell my children again. After a hug from Mrs Binout, she made Matt and myself a cup of tea and remarked on how much weight we'd both lost.

We chatted, unsuccessfully attempting to summarise everything that had happened and then, mugs drained, it was time for Matt to return to his family. After having been so inextricably entangled, it was a wrench to see him depart.

I weighed myself - crikey, I'd lost nearly a stone - then wallowed and soothed my aching joints and sore feet in the bath and reflected for a very long time indeed... only the severe onset of prune-like, wrinkly fingers indicated that it was time to remove myself from the rapidly cooling aqueous retreat.

Back downstairs, I realised that nothing in the house had changed. Yes, there was a pile of post and I had some major unpacking and serious washing to attend to. Other than that, normal life had carried on and everything was still the same - life as normal. But it wasn't though. Because I had conquered Kili and the memories were overflowing inside me and I simply had to tell everyone. Perhaps a leaflet-drop or a newspaper announcement would do the trick. I hadn't yet discovered Facebook.

Soon, though, it was huge hugs and kisses from my excitable kids, home from school. It wouldn't be too long before I would be able to unleash all my tales of conquest and bravery in a mysterious, far-off foreign land before I burst. First though, of course, I had to listen to what was on their personal agendas: who had said what to whom at school, could I help with Maths homework, what could they snack on now, etc, etc.

Eventually, my moment arrived. I had presumed that my two children would listen for all of ten minutes before attentiveness surrendered to the pressure of their friends beckoning on social media. But, to their credit, they very kindly allowed me my moment of glory, didn't glaze over, and asked pertinent questions with genuine interest; what else could they have done when staple-gunned to the wall though? My short-lived moment of being 'Super Dad the Heroic Explorer' eventually expired but there were plenty of others who would soon enjoy (or perhaps 'endure') my ripping yarns.

A few days later, on my first post-trip visit to the school gates, the Head Teacher approached me with a warm smile. He congratulated me on my achievement, thanked me for the money that had been raised for the school and asked if I would be prepared to give a presentation to the whole school at assembly. I tried to 'play it cool' by seemingly casually agreeing to the request but, inwardly, I was so thrilled and excited to have been given the opportunity to demonstrate my bravery to a captive audience. I was sure the school kids wouldn't be glued to the assembly hall floor. I immediately phoned my agent.

The preparation for my school appearance provided the perfect opportunity with which to go through my photographs and diary notes and make complete sense of the trip before time had a chance to begin the process of eroding the vivid memories.

Despite my own two children suffering excruciating embarrassment at me being a 'celebrity guest presenter' (as I was now ironically referring to myself as) at school, the slide-show was very well received and there were many enthusiastic and inquisitive questions, the sorts of which can only emerge from a child's perspective; the toilet facilities, farting, the effects of altitude and Dougie being their favourite subjects to explore further.

Much to my delight, I was even invited back to give a talk to a specific class; they were currently learning about volcanoes. My adventures would provide them with an interesting first-hand account of climbing up a volcano, albeit a dormant one.

During the first few days since my return, I hadn't expected to have been, whilst not exactly tired, in need of so much sleep. In fact, it took two weeks before I felt completely 'normal' by which time no one was particularly interested in my adventure any longer.

For me, however, each and every idle moment was filled with thoughts and memories of the trip. And, of course, they were fuelled by a frenzy of email exchanges and sharing of photos amongst the members of the group. Eventually, even all that activity subsided as normal life prevailed.

I have to confess, I'm hopeless at keeping in touch with people. Is it a bloke thing? Apart from Matt, I am no longer in contact with any of the supposed 'life-long' friends from the Kili-conquering group. And, it's been the same with every adventure since. An incredibly closely-knit group, then... gone. Am I, are we, simply just too busy with 'stuff' to develop and nurture new friendships?

Despite swearing never to go near a mountain ever again, within a month of returning home, I was craving another foreign adventure, preferably with Matt.

I had realised that, on these group trips, the dynamics and interactions between fellow travellers are so important. Of course, almost by definition, everyone is like-minded anyway but I would say, in particular, one's room-mate or tent-mate is a key factor in ensuring all goes as well as possible. You have someone 'on your side', someone to laugh and joke with, particularly when the going gets really tough.

Matt had been the absolute perfect travelling companion and I honestly believe that simply being able to fart, without embarrassment or hesitation, in someone's company as well as sharing a similar sense of humour are true tests of a worthy companion.

True to his word, Matt had dragged me to the top of Kili for which I really did owe him a huge debt of gratitude; he knows that, I've told him enough times. I recalled, back in April in the Brecons, how he'd promised we would summit together. It had seemed a fairly flippant statement at the time. But, actually, as the goal slowly became a distinct possibility and, in particular, once the summit night attempt had been well and truly engaged, Matt had remained with me. I know, had he been on his own, he could have summited a good three weeks before me but, no, he ensured we stuck together all the way to the very top. He wasn't going to let me fail. He didn't. Top bloke!

We still talk about it now, years later. There's a knowing look of appreciation and respect in our eyes whenever we reminisce. It had certainly been my toughest physical and mental challenge by quite some distance. It had taken me to personal boundaries I was completely unaware of and tested me to new levels of endurance I had no idea that I was capable of. And, all of this had been wonderfully tempered by so many tearful laughs, previously unimaginable highs and, of course, my biggest sense of achievement ever. We now have a most treasured shared experience and a special bond which developed over the course of five months' training and was ultimately forged when we stood together on top of Kili. Yes, we really did do it and the memories of our adventure will remain with us always. I suppose that means, as with Asim and Naiman, that I love him too?

Yep! :-)

Epilogue

I really hope you've enjoyed reading about this adventure. You may recall that I initially wrote it as a personal account for family and friends. But then, as a larger project, I wanted it to entertain and inspire. If I've achieved that then I shall consider this book a worthy success.

You may have noticed that I have dedicated this book to some members of my family. They all have something in common. They have each been taken from our world by cancer. No one is unaffected by cancer. Since 2007, the Binouts have had a monthly direct debit set up for a cancer charity. Hopefully, you'll be pleased to learn that, simply by buying a physical copy of this book, an additional modest contribution will be given to this charity for every copy sold.

Danny, the schoolboy who I have mentioned previously in this book, has been given the all clear! Yes, he will still need regular checks but what a wonderful first, small step forward in his recovery. He is an enormously brave boy who, for a time, was removed, far away from routine life. He and his family now deserve some quiet time, as well as continued support, to allow a degree of normality to seep back into their lives. His story, like many other similar ones, puts anything and everything else firmly into perspective.

When I first decided to tackle Kilimanjaro, some people rolled their eyes and described it as a mid-life crisis. I'm not sure I necessarily believe in such a thing. I did, however, take up learning to play the guitar upon my return from Tanzania. Not only has that rewarded me with so much pleasure – unlike for those within earshot – but I feel it's an excellent workout for my brain. 'Use it or lose' really is good advice. Maybe I'll grow a ponytail next and let it trail behind me as I drive in my yet-to-be-bought open top sports car.

My biggest motivation for the trip was simply to try something extraordinarily new and to step far outside my comfort zone while I was still able to. This in turn was largely prompted by the fact that my 'half-time oranges' had been consumed some time ago and I was well into the 'second-half' and, to put it bluntly, the passing away of people I'd known. Perhaps it *was* a form of mid-life crisis.

I don't necessarily subscribe to the 'treat each day as if it's your last' line of thought. It's hardly practical but I understand the sentiment. And, I see far too many people engrossed in the fakery of their phones and social media. Why not experience more authentic life in the now rather than watching it remotely later with detached senses? As far as I'm concerned, life is more about using spare time wisely and productively through the pursuit of new challenges and experiences and to do it *now* if you can. None of us knows what's round the next corner.

The Kilimanjaro trip had not only taken me, literally, thousands of miles outside my comfort zone but it had also acted as an appetiser (strictly speaking, it was probably a rather generous main course) for life's menu should I then choose to dine in that particular restaurant. And that, I suppose, is a pertinent point. A great number of us are lucky enough to be able to make choices and try something new. Do we really take advantage of this? It's never too late, or too soon for that matter.

If I'd failed, yes, I'd have been hugely disappointed but at least I'd have given it a go. I probably would have made a second attempt. And, I have the utmost respect for anyone who steps outside their comfort zone and attempts a new challenge, regardless of the apparent difficulty *and* regardless of the outcome.

Certainly, I now regard my old self, the one who took on the challenge of Kili, with immense pride and a huge sense of achievement. He did really well.

So, go on. Go and try something new. Don't be someone who says they'd 'like to', be a person who 'does'. You'll probably surprise yourself and most likely, one day, sit back and reflect, yes, maybe Binout had a point and I'm really glad I did that.

As for me, well, I'm off on another trip. Maybe our paths will cross...

Appendix

If, specifically, you are considering tackling Kilimanjaro then you might be interested in my own very modest snippets of recommendations. They should, metaphorically, help you on your first few steps. This is all based upon personal experience and I am not sponsored by anyone (I wish I was) so there are no conflicts of interest.

A brilliant book:
Kilimanjaro: The Trekking Guide to Africa's Highest Mountain by Henry Stedman. It's published by Trailblazer Publications and is, at the time of writing, in its 5th revised edition.

A special acknowledgment:
After writing this book I then tentatively contacted Henry Stedman and asked if I could reproduce some of the graphics which appear in his book. He granted me full permission and couldn't have been nicer. I therefore want to fully acknowledge his support.
Kilimanjaro - The Trekking Guide (Trailblazer) © Henry Stedman
www.climbmountkilimanjaro.com

The kit:
Henry, not surprisingly, explores this in his book and your chosen travel company should also provide you with a comprehensive kit list. Between them, you will probably have sufficient advice. However, when I first started to accrue the various items required for the Kilimanjaro trip, I was overwhelmed by the huge array of brands and price ranges on offer. Over the years, I have largely come to the conclusion that price very closely reflects quality and that classic phrase, 'buy cheap, buy twice', certainly rings true. So, from my own experience, I am happy to add:

It's most important to wear a decent pair of, broken-in, boots. I can personally recommend Meindl (they've been making hiking boots for over 300 years) and Salomon (they, meanwhile, have *only* "been playing in the French alps since 1947").

Of equal importance is the sleeping bag. I took a Marmot Never Summer and not once was I cold at night – other than, of course, when popping out for a wee. Which reminds me, a she-wee or he-wee comes highly recommended. As do biodegradable wet wipes. I also took my own toilet paper (and used it) and antibacterial hand gel.

I wore Craghoppers trousers, a Rab® thermal base layer, and a Berghaus fleece top, waterproof and windproof jacket, and fleece hat. For my multi-layer fleece system, I simply went to the cheaper end of the market and bought Regatta, leaving most of those behind with the guides and porters. My wonderfully warm down jacket was from The North Face. For gloves, I wore a cheap, thin inner layer but spent a reasonable amount of money on a pair of cosy, waterproof mittens.

Despite the cold nights you will probably encounter plenty of bright sunshine and will therefore require a sun hat, sun glasses and high factor sun protection.

I took a 35-litre rucksack and I've always been very happy with Lowe Alpine and Osprey brands. Everything inside my rucksack and kit bag was also squeezed into various waterproof stuff sacks for added protection from the elements. It did result in a heck of a lot of packing and unpacking but it was worth it.

Hydration:
I would recommend taking a Camelbak or Platypus system as well as one or two 1-litre aluminium bottles. I also had my own supply of water purification tablets. I'm not sure if they were necessary but I did use them for added peace of mind. Plus, I also used High5 Zero flavoured (grapefruit, since you ask) hydration tablets. Do not takes ones which contain caffeine though, or you may struggle *even more* to get to get to sleep at night.

Electrical:
You will definitely require a head torch and remember spare batteries too. The same will apply to your camera and mobile phone. I also took a solar charger (the ones which are not much bigger than a smart phone as opposed to the larger panel types) which I carried on the outside of my rucksack each day. In the past, I've been very happy with Levin™ and Anker.

For additional record-keeping take a diary, pencil and sharpener.

Medication:
I can only speak for myself on this subject and you **must** consult your own doctor for suitable advice. For me, I used aspirin and paracetamol, and *Diamox* once. On many occasions, I have found COMPEED® blister plasters and their anti-blister stick very useful indeed. The latter on most occasions preventing the use of the former.

Another of Matt's tips:
Don't take a pillow. Simply pack a pillow case and fill that with your fleeces at night. As I discovered on a subsequent trip, it works a treat.

The preparation:
For most of us, it's virtually impossible to train in a high-altitude environment. But it should be possible to do plenty of hiking in mountainous or hilly terrains. I clocked-up just over 200 miles of hiking, prior to travelling to Tanzania, and most of it involved carrying around 6-7kg of weight in my rucksack. That got me suitably mountain-fit. Remember, you will be paying a great deal of money for this once-in-a-lifetime trip so make sure you get fit. Trust me, it will be well worth the effort.

The travel company:
In my travels I have used and can therefore personally recommend:
Exodus Travels (www.exodus.co.uk)
KE Adventure Travel (www.keadventure.com)
G Adventures (www.gadventures.com).
Each of these provide trips to Kilimanjaro.

The route:
Simply put, the more days you spend on the ascent the higher your chances of success are. I've only made one attempt at Kili, using the longest route – Lemosho. I thoroughly enjoyed its varied scenery and environments. There is plenty of information on every single route in Henry's book as well as from the travel companies but do take time to choose which one best fits your parameters.

And finally, but equally as important:
Be prepared to face some very tough times indeed. You will probably suffer from bad headaches and nausea, and lose your appetite. Don't

be too concerned if/when this happens. It's perfectly normal. But, if you've got yourself fit, arrive bursting with your biggest positive mental attitude ever, walk slowly even to the extent of it seeming ridiculously so, consume the recommended 4-5 litres of water each day, look around and appreciate the wonderful environment, talk to and get to know your guides, and can laugh in times of utter despair then you'll stand a very good chance of reaching one of our planet's 'Seven Summits'. How brilliant does that sound! Good luck.

Front cover photograph acknowledgements:
I took hundreds of photos but, at the time, only possessed a cheap camera. So, despite wonderful photographic memories I do not have any of suitable quality for the front cover of this book. Consequently, for the main image, I have used one from the internet:
This Wikipedia and Wikimedia Commons image is from the user Chris 73 and is freely available at:
//commons.wikimedia.org/wiki/File:Uhuru_Peak_Mt._Kilimanjaro_2.JPG under the creative commons cc-by-sa 3.0 license.

The chameleon photograph, under the terms of the cc-by-2.0, is from:
Author: AN Suresh Kumar from Chennai, India
https://upload.wikimedia.org/wikipedia/commons/c/c6/An_Indian_chameleon_wildlife_in_Andhra_Pradesh_India_2016.jpg

Thinking of hiking in Morocco?

I have hiked in the Atlas Mountains and summited the highest peak in North Africa there; Jebel Toubkal or Mount Toubkal.

If you're ever considering a trip to this region, then I cannot recommend highly enough an absolutely brilliant guide - **Mohamed Maachou**

No one has a greater depth of knowledge of this region than Mohamed. He is also one of the nicest people you could ever meet!

www.activetreksmorocco.com
activetreksmorocco@gmail.com

NB Sipping a mint tea, seated high up in the Café de France overlooking Jemaa el-Fnaa square in Marrakesh is a real treat.

Been there, done it, want the Kili t-shirt?

'Kilimanjaro 5895 t shirt'

Available in 5 colours:

UK: www.amazon.co.uk/dp/B07K6YQSMZ
USA: www.amazon.com/dp/B07K6YT1NN
Germany: www.amazon.de/dp/B07K6X9YNB

Also, Pullover Hoodie (one colour)

USA only: www.amazon.com/dp/B07K6X4844

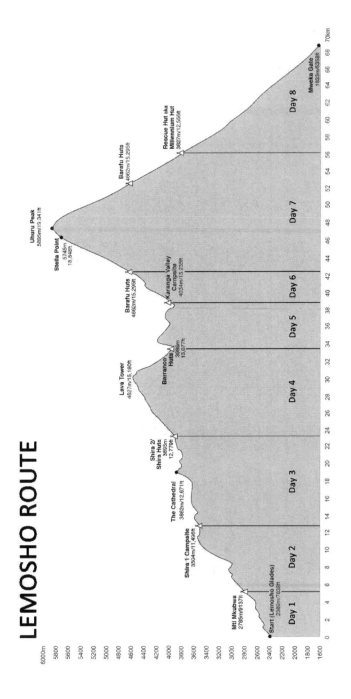

43098835R00123

Printed in Poland
by Amazon Fulfillment
Poland Sp. z o.o., Wrocław